Better Homes and Gardens®

Home improvement book

Contents

Transforming your kitchen into a more efficient, better-looking area, regardless of its size; discussion of three typical kitchen layouts; and ideas for adding storage space, improving lighting, and more.

Plenty of suggestions for updating a bathroom—wall and floor coverings, lighting, built-ins, new fixtures, ventilation, additional storage space, ceiling treatments, shower units, even a sauna.

Finding the space for an additional powder room, ¾ bath, or full bath in the space that you have, in the attic, a hallway, under a stairway, or in a master bedroom closet.

Planning for facilities—carport, detached garage, or attached garage—that will get your car off the street and out of sight, with additional ideas for storage and a workshop.

Ideas and helps for creating outdoor living space, dealing with problem lots, achieving a good landscaping effect, the best materials to use, and installation techniques.

How to make the best use of your basement by converting it into a family room, shop area, or a laundry center. Also, general information on plumbing, venting, water seepage, power requirements, sound, and safety. Plus special ideas that will add a unique touch to your basement.

BETTER HOMES AND GARDENS BOOKS
Editorial Director: Don Dooley
Managing Editor: Malcolm E. Robinson   Art Director: John Berg
Asst. Managing Editor: Lawrence D. Clayton   Asst. Art Director: Randall Yontz
Designers: Harijs Priekulis, Tonya Rodriguez
Contributing Editor: Richard V. Nunn
Technical Editor: Stephen Mead

Introduction

The little guy across the page has just finished reading *Better Homes and Gardens Home Improvement Book,* and he's ready to tackle that project he has been putting off since who knows when. Before, he wasn't sure how to solve his remodeling problem, what materials to use, or where to go for help if he needed it. Now, armed with an arsenal of valuable information and know-how, he's ready.

More than likely, you are in much the same predicament that this fellow was in. You know that your house is not all that you want it to be, and yet, for one reason or another, the project is still there to be done, and you are still thinking about it.

Maybe you want a more efficient kitchen or an updated bathroom or a family room in the basement or additional bedroom space in the attic or a carport or a deck for entertaining outdoors or a winterized porch. Whatever project you've got in mind, *Home Improvement Book* will tell you how best to approach it, how to plan it, and how to execute your plan most efficiently and at the least cost.

At the beginning of each chapter there are three popular projects—for example, in Basement Conversion there is a Laundry Center, Shop Area, and a Family Room that you can fit into the basement. Often there is a 'before' and 'after' view of the project.

This is followed by a section that provides you with both planning and buymanship—what you can

do in a certain size house, the common pitfalls to avoid, the materials you *can* and *cannot* use, where to get specialized information and help for that extraordinary problem. You'll find information about walls—what to do with them, how to decorate them with paper, paint, or paneling, and ideas about unusual wall treatments. You'll find, also, information about ceilings and floors, including specific how-to-prepare information.

Other data in each of these sections zeros in on some basic how-to techniques that you may apply to any number of small-to-large fix-up or remodeling jobs. For example, the concrete methods explained in the chapter on patios and decks also applies to driveways and walks.

The last section of each chapter is devoted to photographs of specific ideas that you can use in your home improvement project—maybe a fireplace in your basement, storage ideas for the kitchen, a sauna in the bathroom.

By the time you have studied the chapter that deals with the project you're interested in, you'll be able to tell an architect, building contractor, or builder exactly what you want. Use the *Home Improvement Book* properly and you'll have no difficulty doing that project you've put off since you bought your home. Best yet, you may be able to do lots of the work yourself and save money.

Kitchen Remodeling

Don't just put up with your kitchen. Transform it into a hardworking, good-looking service center. If there are things that you don't like about it, change them. Get that wall or floor covering you've had your eye on. Improve the lighting if it isn't serving your needs. Add more storage space. You can do all these things and more—easily and inexpensively.

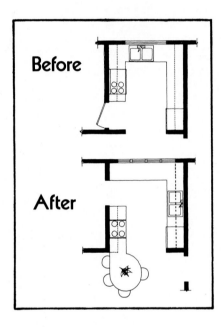

Before

After

U-Shaped Kitchen

Of the three most popular kitchen layouts—U-shaped, L-shaped, and galley—the U-shaped kitchen is the most efficient. There are good reasons for this. Because of its shape, work flow is not interrupted by unwanted traffic; there is a minimum of wasted steps between the various work centers; and there is ample work space because cabinets are continuous.

The typical U-shaped kitchen has the sink at the base of the U and the refrigerator and the range on either side. This allows the work to flow smoothly from the refrigerator to the sink to the range.

Remember that for a U-shaped kitchen you'll need at least eight feet in width to make the kitchen work for you. Many people run into trouble with the U-shaped kitchen because they try to squeeze it into too small an area. If this happens, only one person at a time can work in the kitchen.

Generally, U-shaped kitchens are short on natural light, and few are big enough for an eating area. Light presents no special problems because you can simply add more windows, as was done in this kitchen remodeling project.

However, to gain eating space, you'll have to open up the kitchen to either a family room or dining room. This was accomplished in this kitchen by knocking out the wall between the kitchen and family room. Then, the entrance to the dining room was relocated and the range and counters were moved closer to the family room. Notice how the addition of a breakfast bar joins the two areas together. In this case, the sink was brought up closer to the family room to preserve the compact work-flow pattern.

L-Shaped Kitchen

Naturally, the bigger the kitchen, the better. The trouble is, most kitchens just aren't big enough. So how do you get the most use out of existing space? Consider an L-shaped kitchen in your remodeling plans.

A great many good things can be said for the L-shaped layout. For one, the work centers take up very little space, often leaving enough room for a dining area. For another, this plan is efficient, resulting in very few wasted steps. Also, you won't be bothered by unwanted traffic because of the smooth sequence between activity centers. If planned with care, this kitchen can accommodate two cooks.

One word of caution: if either of the sections of the L would be shorter than eight feet long, use another plan. With any less footage than this, the appliances will eat up most of the space, leaving you with very little work area, which is so badly needed.

Before

After

Remodeling this L-shaped kitchen resulted in an improved traffic pattern, more counter and storage space, and a new entrance into the dining room. The wall between the kitchen and dining room was knocked out, and a work island was added to the counter. In addition, the refrigerator and the range changed positions, making for a more logical work flow. Closet with sliding doors provides much-needed storage for cleaning equipment.

Because galley kitchens are open at both ends, excessive traffic is often a problem. Naturally, the easiest solution is to close off one end. The approach taken in this kitchen was to wall up the end nearest the dining room, leaving a pass-through for ease in serving. In addition, the wall behind the range was knocked out, making room for an eating bar opposite the range. The eating bar is a convenient place for youngsters' after-school snacks or a quick breakfast before work or play.

Additional windows were installed to achieve more natural light.

Before

After

Galley Kitchen

If your kitchen is a runway of activity, the galley (corridor) layout is not for you. However, if you're not faced with this problem, this plan might be just right for your kitchen. Characterized by a double row of cabinets flanking an aisle, this plan is most efficient when the refrigerator, sink, and mix centers line one wall; the cooking and serving areas, the other. In addition, try to keep the counters as close to each other as possible so as to achieve a compact work pattern.

The galley plan is ideal for combining the kitchen with the adjoining dining room. When one of the work walls is open above the base cabinets, you have a ready-made serving counter, plus a divider between the rooms. This arrangement comes in handy especially when you are entertaining. You won't have to carry the food very far, and cleanup is easy and can be taken care of quickly. Besides, your guests won't be distracted by a messy kitchen. The pass-through arrangement could even be shuttered to screen the entire room.

Select the Right Materials

It's not surprising that kitchen remodeling is the No. 1 home improvement. This is the area where the family gathers together, and where the homemaker spends so much of her time. What is surprising, however, is how easily and inexpensively you can remodel a kitchen. More often than not, simply making a few minor changes will yield a much better looking and more efficient kitchen.

Whether you are considering laying new flooring, giving your walls a new treatment, installing countertops/backsplashes or cabinets, or improving the lighting, wiring, or ventilation, you must know what materials are most suitable for the project, where to go for advice if you need it, and how to plan your remodeling wisely.

Floor coverings: Often, a new floor covering is all that is needed to make your kitchen come alive. Whether you decide on tile and sheet goods, carpeting, or one of the rigid materials, purchase the best quality you can afford, for only a quality material will stand up under the heavy traffic in your kitchen.

Tile and sheet goods: These floor coverings are popular with many do-it-yourselfers. Tiles are especially easy to install, either by cementing them in place or by simply positioning those with a self-adhesive backing. Sheets, although a little harder to work with because of their size, result in a seamless floor—a real plus when it comes to maintenance.

Vinyl, the most popular floor covering available for kitchens, is relatively inexpensive and easy to maintain. But there are more reasons to proclaim vinyl's virtues—it is long-lasting, resilient, and resistant to almost everything.

Sheet vinyl, also a good floor covering to use in the kitchen, rates excellent in all categories. One asset that particularly attracts people to sheet vinyl is the wide selection of patterns available.

If you're looking for a comfortable floor covering for your kitchen, none can compare to cushioned sheet vinyl. Although more ex-pensive than some of the other floor coverings, its superior resilience and excellent resistance to grease and stains, plus the long wear and ease of maintenance, will make your investment a wise one.

Another well-liked kitchen floor covering, vinyl asbestos tile, rates excellent in all categories, with the exception of having only fair resilience. Because of its low cost, it's a good choice if you're on a limited budget. Consider installing it yourself to save money.

The most expensive tile floor covering, solid vinyl tile, has outstanding characteristics—durability and ease of maintenance. Although only fairly resilient, solid vinyl is worth the price you'll pay for it.

Rotovinyl appeals to many people because it resembles cushioned sheet vinyl, yet it costs less. Other desirable characteristics include excellent resilience; excellent resistance to grease, alkalies, and stains; and ease of maintenance with just a damp mopping.

Cork tile and its cousin, vinyl cork tile, are quiet underfoot and are easy to maintain. Although these tiles are rather expensive, their resilience rates very good, and they will last for years with proper care.

Rubber tile will hold up under heavy use for a long time. And it's comfortable underfoot. However, there are two things to keep in mind if you decide on rubber tile: it is very slippery when wet; and there are not many colors from which to choose.

Asphalt tile, the least expensive floor covering, is difficult to maintain because of its poor soil resistance. For this reason, you'll be better off not using it.

Seamless vinyl poured floors are most useful if your floors are uneven. The endless design possibilities are their most notable feature. Cleanup is a snap because dirt and dust have no place to hide.

Carpeting: There has long been much discussion as to whether or not carpeting has a rightful place in the kitchen. Some people insist that because the kitchen is a heavy traffic area, no carpeting, regardless of its quality, can withstand the use for long. Others are equally insistent that carpeting is the best of all the floor coverings.

Actually, neither of these positions is correct. It is true that the kitchen is one area in your home with an immense amount of traffic. However, because good-quality carpeting has excellent resilience, resists grease, alkalies, and stains, is quiet and comfortable underfoot, and is relatively easy to maintain, it is a good choice for some kitchens.

When selecting carpeting, make sure that you get quality goods. Trim-tufted carpeting with short dense loops is the easiest type to maintain. The best soil concealers are the medium golds, browns, greens, and blues.

Kitchen carpeting is available in 6-, 9-, and 12-foot widths and also in tile form. Tiles are adhesive-backed, so they are easy for the do-it-yourselfer to lay.

Caution: Kitchen carpeting will cause you much work and will not stand up well under certain conditions. For example, if your kitchen is close to an outside door, you'll constantly be plagued by dirt and dust that people carry in on their shoes. Children, too, can be hard on carpeting because of their uncanny ability to spill things on the floor. Even pets, such as cats or dogs, will make new carpeting look old in a hurry. Consider this in your planning.

Rigid materials: These include hard and soft woods, brick, and ceramic tile, plus several others. As most of these floorings are not commonplace in kitchens, you may wish to capitalize on this to achieve a unique kitchen area that will surely dazzle people when they see the floor for the first time.

One thing to consider if you are contemplating a rigid flooring is that they are permanent. So, if you are unsure about whether or not you will be moving in the near future, or if you're not certain that you'll like the rigid material for a long time, decide whether the relatively high cost of rigid floorings will be offset by the beauty they offer.

Wood floors, if they are protected with clear plastic or several coats of wax, are both handsome and practical in kitchens. However, wood is slippery and demands care to retain its beauty. Also, moisture and changes in temperature will cause wood to swell and shrink, leaving cracks in which dust and dirt can collect. There are a great many precut shapes and types available.

Brick floors can be exceptionally attractive, especially if you have a country kitchen. Brick maintains easily if properly sealed, and is long-wearing. And although it is not the most comfortable floor covering available, you may decide to sacrifice some comfort underfoot for durability.

Ceramic tile is one of the most sturdy floor coverings available. In addition, it comes in a variety of patterns and colors, and is easily maintained. You can purchase ceramic tile in glazed or unglazed form, but for kitchen use, the glazed works best. It can be rather expensive, especially if you have it installed by professional tile setters.

Wall coverings: If chosen wisely, these add to your kitchen. If you're like most other people, the first thing that comes to mind is paint. But don't forget two other wall treatments that can also give your walls new life—wallpaper and paneling.

Paint: Without a doubt, painting your kitchen walls is the fastest, most economical, and easiest way to alter the appearance of your kitchen. Paint also provides you with many color possibilities.

Besides deciding on which color works best for you, you will also need to consider what type of paint to use. An enamel paint is a must for long-lasting good looks. One with either an oil or water base will usually suffice for most kitchen walls. Oil-base enamel is impervious to almost everything and is very durable. Water-base enamel, on the other hand, leaves no odor, dries quickly, and washes out of paintbrushes easily with soapy water.

If you're unsure about the type of paint to use in your kitchen, go to a paint store for help. If you have problem walls or excess moisture, for example, the salesperson will be able to suggest the right paint for your wall.

Wallpaper: If your remodeling plans call for applying some wallpaper, make sure to select a paper that will hold up for a long time and one that is easy to care for. Your best bet for kitchen use is one of the vinyl papers. Available in a wide variety of flocked, wet-look, wood grain, and textured patterns, vinyl wallpaper comes plain-backed or prepasted. The prepasted type must be soaked in water to activate the paste, so it's about as easy, and less expensive, to apply paste with a wide brush to the plain-backed type.

Once installed, vinyl wallpaper is easy to care for. If grease or dirt collect on the paper, simply wipe with a damp cloth.

Measuring for wallpaper isn't hard because each roll contains 35 square feet. However, if measurements aren't your forte, simply determine the size of your kitchen and take the dimensions to a wallpaper dealer. He'll be glad to help you determine your needs.

Paneling: Although suitable for any kitchen walls, paneling becomes especially good if you have problem walls—those with several layers of wallpaper or badly cracked or chipped plaster. Not only does paneling add to the value of your home, it is easily installed and quite durable.

As with paint and wallpaper, paneling can be applied to all of the walls or used selectively. Unlike the above, two, paneling is a one-application job. If you're wondering about whether you can find just what you want, rest easy because paneling comes in a variety of materials—solid wood, plywood with surface veneers, plastic-surfaced hardboard, even wallboard with simulated wood patterns.

Plastic-laminated paneling, one of the more recent innovations in paneling, is achieving popularity quickly. It's even better in kitchens than wood paneling because the baked-on plastic finish makes for easy maintenance. Dirt and grease cause no problem; simply wipe clean with a damp cloth. And you'll never need to worry about fading or discoloration for years into the future.

This type of paneling comes in 4x8-foot panels. It is easy to install; you can cut the panels to fit with a fine-toothed saw blade. A special waterproof adhesive ensures against damage from moisture.

A word of caution: With the exception of plastic-laminated paneling, don't use paneling where the danger of moisture exists. Moisture will cause the paneling to warp or buckle. Also make sure that your paneling has been treated with a sealing compound.

Countertops: They tend to be ignored by many people who think that once a countertop is installed, that's it. Actually, if you've got the know-how, you can redo any countertop with relative ease. However, if you have a plastic laminate countertop, you'll be ahead headache-wise if you call a professional.

The countertop choices available to you are many. Choose from linoleum, laminated plastic (either in sheet form or post-formed), vinyl, ceramic tile, hardwood (chopblock), or stainless steel. Or use a combination of these.

Should you decide to install a new countertop and backsplash yourself, make sure that the subcounter is structurally sound. There are two common types of subcounters: those made of plywood and those made of stripping. Plywood may delaminate when you remove the old countertop, so you might need to put on new plywood. If your subcounter is made of stripping, it may have buckled in which case you should put on new stripping.

Cabinets: In most kitchens, these are at a premium. There just never seem to be enough of them to house all of the food preparation equipment and supplies necessary for food preparation. So, what do you do if you're faced with this problem? You have two options: custom-built cabinets or factory-built ones.

Custom-built cabinets: These offer the tremendous advantage of being tailor-made to your needs. If you know exactly what types of cabinets you want, but you don't know how to build them, hire a cabinetmaker to build to your specifications. On the other hand, if you enjoy carpentry and are good at it, consider building your own.

Factory-built cabinets: These cabinets come in many sizes, shapes, designs, and materials. So that you can get a good idea of what is available, go to a local kitchen supply dealer and inspect his lines. The dealer will be happy to answer any questions and to help you decide on just the right cabinets. These cabinets are easy for the handyman to install. You can buy either wood or metal ones.

Good lighting and wiring: These are a must in today's kitchens. If you have these two things, your kitchen will be a bright, cheery area in which to work—and a safe one.

Achieve efficient lighting by combining general background illumination and localized lighting. Both incandescent and fluorescent lighting are good in kitchens, so deciding which one to use is a matter of personal preference. Remember that the work centers and the eating area should be especially well lit. Also keep in mind that if the ceiling is light-colored, you'll need less light than if the ceiling is covered with a dark material.

If you're unsure about your wiring needs, contact your local utility company or an electrical contractor. Either will analyze your situation and recommend needed changes.

Adequate ventilation: This can cure many kitchen ills—grease, impurities, and odor. To achieve efficient ventilation, you must have a fan that will change the air at least 15 times an hour. There are two types of ventilating fans: ducted and ductless. The ducted type is best because it vents impurities to the outside. But a ductless hood with a fan and a filter will trap most contaminants and recycle the air.

Design, construction, and materials sources: Whenever you're in doubt about any aspect of your kitchen remodeling project, consult a specialist in the field. Many home improvement contractors are specialists in kitchen remodelings.

For design help consult a kitchen design service, an architect, a designer, or a local utility. Another good source of design help is the Council of Kitchen Designers, 199 Main Street, Hackettstown, New Jersey 07840. Asking questions beforehand will save you money in the long run.

Construction help is easy to come by—just make sure that you talk to the right person. Kitchen remodelers, a reliable supply dealer, or a remodeling contractor are experts in this field, and should be able to give you all of the help you need.

When it comes to materials sources, check with a nearby lumberyard, flooring and wall covering companies, and appliance dealers. Catalog stores are a good source, too.

Planning: You'll save irritation if you plan in advance of your remodeling. Here are a few things to consider about cabinets and counter space.

There are two types of cabinets: base and wall. The standard height of base cabinets is 34½ inches; standard depth is 24 inches. Wall cabinets are usually 13 inches deep and 32 inches high. The top of the wall cabinets should be 84 inches from the floor. Allow 15 inches between counter and wall cabinets.

Counter tops are most often 36 inches high. For optimum efficiency in your kitchen, you'll need some counter space beside each work center. Beside the refrigerator plan for at least 1½ feet of counter space. At the range 2 feet is generally sufficient. Three feet on either side of the sink is best. And beside the mixing area plan to have at least 4 feet.

Glossary

Backsplash—wall covering between base and wall cabinets; should be impervious to water.

Bulkhead—built-out section between the wall cabinets and the ceiling.

Plastic laminate—material often used for counter tops and backsplashes.

Post-formed counter—a factory-made counter that is ready to install.

Radiant heating—a method of heating, usually with coils or pipes placed or embedded in a floor, wall, or ceiling structure.

Rubber emulsion paint—has rubber or synthetic rubber in a water base.

Self edge—the way that plastic laminates are installed to eliminate need for trim pieces.

Toe space—indented space at base of cabinet between the floor and the base cabinets.

Vermiculite—is a type of insulation material. It is a mineral related to mica. It sometimes is used as an aggregate in acoustical plaster.

Wainscoting—matched lumber or panels used to cover the lower part of a wall.

Work triangle—the orderly arrangement of work centers, which makes for efficiency in the basic kitchen layout.

Ideas at a Glance

The size of your kitchen doesn't make it efficient or inefficient. Rather, it's how you put existing space to work. With this in mind, consider the following ideas, and discover how easy it is to gain valuable space in your present kitchen without too much expense.

The modular wall unit shown in the photo below makes very good use of existing space. You can store things in it, serve food from it, eat at it, and so forth. And because of the simple design, this project is within the realm of the handyman. Use A-C grade plywood, and for the counter surfaces, plastic laminate. When not in use, the serving counter and support fold down. Notice, too, that all of the shelves are adjustable. The corkboard wall serves as a bulletin board. Finish the unit with semigloss paint.

The core kitchen pictured above is every bit as convenient as your present kitchen, yet it measures only 5x7 feet. Two things make this concept practical: compact appliances and a service core that consolidates all wiring, plumbing, drain, and gas lines in one hookup and service area.

The mobile appliances fit nicely under the glass-ceramic work top, which extends all the way around the island. The work top is heat/moisture-proof, too, adding to its value.

The arrangement of the food preparation centers makes for a good work flow pattern. Only a few feet separate conventional and microwave ovens from the sink and refrigerator.

And you won't have to worry about having enough storage space with this kitchen. The entire top section of the unit is devoted to storage. Notice, too, that there's even a niche for holding your spices in an organized fashion.

The portable dishwasher and the trash compactor simplify cleanup a great deal. When you're through with a meal, put the dirty dishes into the dishwasher (it is front-loading), and dispose of trash in the compactor.

Here's a nifty idea that will save you a lot of steps at mealtime. Store your condiments in the tri-level mini pantry, so if you forget to set something on the table, you won't have to keep getting up and down. Make the cabinet out of plywood and cover the front with plastic laminate.

An eating booth like the one pictured above can be tailor-made to fit almost any kitchen. This one is made of natural pine and has a plastic laminate tabletop. For added convenience, install an electrical outlet nearby. The light fixture provides good localized light.

This work island with attached eating counter combines beauty with function. The island virtually eliminates cluttered counter tops and also makes it possible for two cooks to work in the kitchen at the same time. The eating counter is the perfect place to serve breakfasts, lunches, or after-school snacks.

The handy storage shelf pictured below houses a variety of often-used items in a convenient place. Make the unit from 1x8s and 1x2 facing strips at either end and in the center. The dividers are ¼-inch hardboard. Insert a one-inch dowel on the right side for paper towels. Hinge 1x8 doors to the shelf, and attach chains.

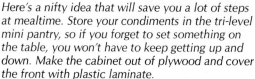

Use ¼-inch oak plywood and edging tape to make this compact spice rack/work counter. The counter folds down, and the support, mounted with a piano hinge, swings flat. Hinge counter on bottom shelf. Shelves are 24 inches wide and six inches high. Finish with stain or paint.

Here's a novel storage idea that puts the space between the counter top and cabinets to work (right). Use 1x6s to form compartments for items such as glasses, a blender, salad bowls, or mixing spoons. Then join the boxes with butt joints, glue, and nails. Either paint unit to match cabinets or use a contrasting color.

This roll-out pastry cart will prove invaluable on baking day. Simply bring it out of its hiding place among the cabinets, lock the wheel brakes, and shape pastry dough anywhere in the kitchen. Its non-stick marble top is excellent for this purpose. The same cart will double as a serving cart. Or pull up a chair and eat at it.

This versatile unit serves as a work area, dining table, and a planning desk. And it occupies very little space. Use a cantilevered brace to support the plastic laminate counter. Then add shelves above the counter to store cook books, recipe files, and knickknacks. Here, the light fixture above the counter ensures well-balanced lighting.

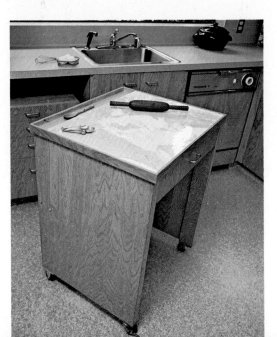

Bathroom Remodeling

You'll be surprised how easy it is to switch one or more fixtures, make needed changes in the lighting, tile or carpet the floor, or add convenient storage space in your bathroom. You already have the basics: wiring and plumbing. First, pick a plan that will work well for your particular situation; then, design yourself a brighter and more functional bathroom.

Left-Hand Plumbing

Few rooms in your home utilize components as well as the bathroom, since most bathroom products come in a 'package': ready-built lavatory/cabinet combinations, bath/shower units, and prepasted wall and floor coverings in handy sheet form. Best yet, the products are relatively inexpensive and easy to install. Left- and right-hand plumbing refers to location of the piping system.

Only a couple of basic changes are needed to create a brand-new mood in your bathroom: a built-in, single basin lavatory with plenty of storage space below simply hooks to a wall; color-coordinated wall coverings go up fast; and sparkling hardware—towel bars and plumbing fixtures—usually require just a screwdriver to put up. Even a new toilet or bathtub is a simple matter of disconnect/connect. You may want a pro to do this.

Look familiar? This bathroom is typical of many pre-1960 houses, complete with chrome-legged lavatory and clinical, sterile-looking floor, walls, and ceiling. Updating the look is not difficult. Simply purchase tailor-made components you can use throughout the bathroom.

The same bathroom was transformed with moisture-tolerant wall coverings and carpeting. The owner also added a prefabbed lavatory unit, which includes single-basin vanity top and cabinets. A soffit was added above the lavatory and tub with light lenses of plastic. Soffit was formed with 2x4s and skinned with ⅝-inch gypsum wallboard panels. Mirror adds the look of space.

This pleasing bathroom started off as a stark room with inadequate storage units. To accommodate indirect lighting, the ceiling was dropped several inches. Fiberboard insets are moisture-resistant; the plastic panes diffuse the light, making it consistent throughout the room.

Structural plastic panels were used for the divider and the window covering; the color tone of the plastic was picked up for the walls and ceiling panels. The vanity is prefabricated and is fastened directly to the wall. The vanity top is made of plastic laminate in marble pattern.

Wasted space and poor lighting were the two bad features of the bathroom. The window, although adequate, created drafts. Nothing had to be changed structurally to remodel the space. The lavatory, toilet, and tub/shower area was simply 'compartmentalized' to take advantage of the space. The same piping was utilized for the lavatory and toilet.

Right-Hand Plumbing

Because of existing space limitations, as a rule, it is best to tie a bathroom remodeling design together with repetition of materials. Splitting up the room with different colors, textures, and gimcracks only segments it. A case in point is this bathroom remodeling where the repeated design of the backsplash tile, toilet, and lavatory is a single element.

Color plays an important role, too. Light colors will make a small room appear larger, although, in a bathroom, you might consider accent walls in a vivid color to add warmth to hard ceramics and laminates.

Lighting also is important. Here, concealed lighting above a new suspended ceiling was utilized. It compensates for the loss of daylight through the bathroom's small window, which is now hidden by a panel of colored structural glass. The room actually looks larger because the lavatory/cabinet combination fills one wall and a new tub/shower unit fills the wasted space along the other wall. Design ties the two together.

Long, Narrow Bath

A bedraggled bathroom can sink your morale, whether you are in a frantic morning rush or a leisure-time soaking period in a warm tub after a hard day's work or play. Smart, new fixtures and dabs of bright color can quickly change the picture. Or, for those on a budget, just a new coat of paint and a change of bathroom hardware put it in focus. The cost may be as little as $25—if you contribute the labor.

This remodeling involved new fixtures—about a three-hour job—and a built-in lavatory with a prefabricated cabinet and lavatory counter top. The ceiling was dropped over the tub, giving the boxy bathroom a new architectural slant without changing it structurally. For more privacy, a swing-out louvered window shutter hides the outside view; yet, it permits light and ventilation.

This long, narrow bathroom (above) with outdated fixtures at one end presents a remodeling problem. The window doesn't help its looks, either, splitting up the wall area and making decorating a problem. The difference in textures and color also added to the confusion in the bathroom.

One solution: paint the rear wall an eye-catching color and repaint the outside of the tub to match. And color-coordinate the carpet with accessories. This would tie the whole room together. New hardware would help the overall appearance, too.

The answer here was more elaborate— new fixtures and color accent (right). Base of the lavatory counter top is ¾-inch exterior plywood. It's covered with plastic laminate, manufactured to specifications in a millwork shop. The cabinet, bathtub, toilet, and mirror are all standard; the carpeting was removed and the hardwood floor refinished with stain. New hardware was also installed.

Select the Right Materials

Since most bathrooms are relatively small in space as compared to other rooms in your home, the key to remodeling them successfully is to preplan the design. Measurements are critical here—more so than in any other room in your home. For example, you can't put a six-foot bathtub in 5½ feet of space—unless you change a wall or rearrange the structural members in the room.

Remember, too, that bathrooms are damp. You must choose materials that are moisture-resistant. There are plenty on the market, so this shouldn't be a problem for you.

A real boon to bathroom remodeling has been the acceptance of component parts. Since most components are prefabricated, you can easily make correct measurements and rearrange the units to fit the space you have to fill. But don't forget doorways and area-ways through which these prefabbed parts have to pass. Also, consider 'working space' with the components. Do you have enough room to install them properly?

Plumbing and wiring in a bathroom are to your advantage; both are already installed. As a rule, it is not difficult to rewire a lighting fixture or disconnect and reconnect a lavatory, toilet, or bathtub. If you feel you don't have the know-how to do this work, call in a professional. You can do the preliminary work; it shouldn't be cost-prohibitive to have a professional make the connections.

Building codes in your area may dictate what you may or may not do in a bathroom remodeling—more than any other room in your home because sanitary conditions are involved. Be sure you check with your municipal building department before you start any work that involves structural changes and plumbing and wiring connections. You may have to have a permit to do this work.

Flooring materials: Those you select must be moisture-resistant because of the dampness problem in the bathroom. There are a lot of materials from which to choose.

Carpeting: Indoor/outdoor carpet and carpet tiles may be used in the bathroom. Also available are moisture-resistant carpeting fabrics that may be washed. The key is to buy carpeting that will withstand the moisture.

If you decide on carpeting, make sure the floor underneath it is in good condition. Any water that soaks through the carpeting may cause structural damage to the floor, subflooring, and joists below.

As a check of the condition of the floor, stick a pen knife through the flooring at the floor joints. If the blade of the knife penetrates the joints easily, the floor may be water-damaged. Also, check below the floor, if at all possible. Water streaks sometimes indicate water damage from above.

Tile: You have two basic choices for use in the bathroom. Resilient tile includes vinyl-asbestos, solid vinyl, rubber, and carpet tiles. Non-resilient tile includes ceramic, slate, and hardwood or parquet-type blocks.

Although there are just two basics, the range of patterns and colors is wide. You may buy tiles that are self-sticking, or standard types that you set yourself. If you choose the latter, make sure you use waterproof adhesive. The subfloor must be in good condition, properly sealed, and clean before any tile is layed. Be sure there are no humps, bumps, or dents. These will show up in the finished flooring.

You may use sheet vinyl and linoleum in bathrooms, too. These are layed over the same underlayment conditions as tile counterparts. But there are specific instructions to follow; ask the dealer for help.

Wood: Wood flooring may be used in a bathroom, but, because of moisture, it is best to consider another type covering. If you do want wood, however, the surface must be thoroughly sealed with a good penetrating stain with top coats of moisture-resistant finish such as urethane. Don't use wood for shower floors.

Paint: A painted bathroom floor is not a wise choice, since moisture may cause the paint to peel and crack. Use ceramic tile, instead.

Wall treatments: Walls, too, are affected by the moisture in a bathroom. So, even though you can't avoid moisture completely, you can choose materials that help control it.

Moisture may rot away the plaster or gypsum wallboard underbase in a very insidious way: you may not even notice that the walls are crumbling under the present wall covering —probably plastic or metal tile. This is especially true if your house is more than 10 years old. Pull off several tiles to check.

The selection of wall covering materials is tremendous: vinyls, wallpaper, paneling, ceramic tile, paint, simulated brick and stone, plastic laminated panels, aluminum sheets, fabric attached to hardboard, plywood, metal, plastic and decorative gypsumboard.

Before you select any material, check the soundness of the walls. If they are crumbling underneath the present covering, you may have to replace the damaged spots.

Plaster can be patched easily. Sections of gypsum wallboard may be cut out and replaced by a new piece. Here, you should use gypsum wallboard that is covered with a plastic-type paper. The joints should be taped, as standard, for a smoother job. If the wall is plaster, patch the damaged area with spackling compound or gypsum wallboard cement, smoothing it level with the rest of the wall. An edge of a 1x3 will make a good guide for this level. Make sure it is straight.

Around a tub/shower combination and over a lavatory where moisture vapor is always present, you should use hardcoat materials such as ceramic tile or plastic laminate. These materials can be easily sandwiched in as color accents to the rest of your room decoration. Do not use linoleum in or around the tub/shower area, since it can be water-damaged.

Fixtures: A new lavatory, bathtub, and a shower are not as costly as you might think. And, best yet, these bathroom components are not difficult to install. All you need is a pipe wrench, propane torch, and some sealing compound. Before any connections are made, turn off the water at the main valve. Disassemble the old; assemble the new. If you don't have the know-how, pay a plumber to do this for you.

If your decorating plans call for white fixtures, be sure that they are acid-resistant. Usually, colored fixtures have the acid-resistant feature built into them. Good fixtures are built on a cast-iron base and don't give when you press on them. The exception to this, of course, is built-in ceramic fixtures. If the fixtures have a resilient feeling to the push, they may not be adequate. Also, keep in mind that old fixtures have to be removed and new ones moved in. Do you have enough door and hallway space to do this?

Storage: It's always important, and usually overlooked in a bathroom. You can buy prefabbed storage units for a bathroom. Be sure they are moisture-treated. Installation is simply a matter of hooking the cabinets to a wall —usually on a 1x4 that has been mounted to the wall with toggle bolts or expansion anchors, or nailed directly to the studs.

Counter tops may be a problem—especially if you want to add special color to the room. You can have a local millwork shop fabricate the counter tops to complement the room. The cost is not prohibitive.

There are many types of bathroom cabinets on the market—ready for installation. You may even use a piece of unfinished furniture for a cabinet, adapting it with coats of moisture-resistant finish. Don't overlook a millwork manufacturer for special orders; you may even find one through a building materials outlet.

Counter tops are easy to order through a building materials supplier; if you don't have the know-how with contact adhesives, have a millwork shop do the work. This may save you money in the long run, as you can spoil a sheet of plastic laminate by setting it on a wooden base incorrectly.

Details and appointments: These can add significantly to your bathroom. Lighting should be decorative and functional.

You can create space with lighting, set a mood, or add special centers. If your bathroom remodeling will consist of compartmentalized units, light each of these separately.

A general rule of thumb is to keep the lighting low, but even, for the entire space. Use at least five 60-watt bulbs or five 20-watt fluorescent tubes for a small bathroom. Also add special lighting for the mirror in the room.

A small soffit over the mirror or makeup area may concentrate light, providing good overall illumination. Here, the light must be directed toward the person using the mirror—not toward the mirror. It should be soft in quality and diffused so it doesn't have any glare or shadows. If wall fixtures are involved, place them about six feet from the floor on each side of the mirror area. They should be about 30 inches apart. If an overhead fixture is used, make this in the center of the mirror and out about 12 to 18 inches from the wall. If you can't put the fixture on the wall, use a ceiling fixture. It should be fluorescent and at least two feet long. Choose a fluorescent light that is flattering to skin tones; some of these produce a cold, hard look.

If your remodeling plan calls for either a dropped or suspended ceiling, install lights in some of the panel areas, using a plastic-type lens as a light diffuser. The distance between the lens and ceiling shouldn't be more than two times the distance between the tubes and the ceiling.

Other lighting considerations include heat lamps and ozone lamps to freshen air.

Ventilation: This is a must in your bathroom. If the bathroom has a window, it should be about 15 percent of the total floor area of the room. Should your plans call for closing the window, you'll need a ventilating fan, properly vented. It should change the air in the room about 12 times per hour. This will be computed for you, usually, by the dealer.

Exhaust fans may be combined with a lighting fixture and/or heat lamp. Buy a quiet-running fan and wire it with a single switch. You should consult your local building code department for hookup specifications and permission to do the job according to specs.

Design help: For many bathroom remodeling projects, this comes from magazines and books. However, if your project is complicated, seek the advice of a good architect or a builder who has a planner or architect on the staff. The cost is about 10 percent of the total project. Another good source is your local building

supply retailer. He not only has the materials, but he may provide you with names of reputable contractors.

Materials help: Your local building materials retailer or major catalog merchandisers probably can supply all of your needs. Too, contact the local chapter of the Home Improvement Council. If you *do* contract for outside help, *do not sign any paper* until you have looked over prices and construction details. Also, make sure you understand the financing charges—interest rate and so forth —before you sign.

Glossary

Component—any piece of building material that has been prefabricated. Good examples of components are a cabinet, a shower unit, and a ceiling system.

Condensation—drops of water that form on the warm side of an exterior surface.

Cove molding—is three sided and has a concave face. Used as baseboard in baths.

Molly bolt—a flange-type bolt for hanging objects to 'hollow' walls. The shank flanges out to hug the backside of the wall.

Plastic laminate—trade name is Formica. It may be used for most counter tops, and, in some cases, as a wall covering or a covering for cabinet fronts. Also used in showers.

Soffit—a lowered ceiling over a tub, shower, or lavatory installation or counter.

Suspended ceiling—a ceiling that is lowered from an existing ceiling by means of metal hangers, channels, and inserts.

Specifications—written details or directions of building. To specify a certain material for construction use.

Toggle bolt—a 'winged' type fastener for hollow wall construction . To use the toggle, you drill a hole in the wall, insert the bolt through the object you want to hang, screw on the flange part, and insert it in the hole.

Undercoating—usually a coating or primer applied to a surface before finishing coats are applied. It could be the first of two or the second of three coats of paint. Undercoating also applied to some sealers for asphalt and concrete surfaces.

Ideas at a Glance

Even on a limited budget, you can update your bathroom into one of the beauties on these pages. Shelves are plastic-covered plywood; box-type shelving is exterior plywood screwed and glued into boxes and painted. The sauna is prefabbed, as is the shower.

The look of space is achieved in this bathroom (right) with a wall-wide mirror and illuminated grid ceiling that diffuses the light in a very soft, glare-free pattern. Moisture-resistant paneling was used to tie the room into a unit. The counter is high-pressure laminate glued to plywood with contact adhesive.

The makeup mirror is nothing but a shadow box of ¾-inch exterior plywood with lights installed over a wall mirror (below). Doors on the small cabinet below are ¼-inch tempered hardboard. These slide in dados cut in top and bottom plywood pieces. The unit extends to floor around lavatory. It is screwed to the wall with angle-iron brackets.

A series of plywood boxes were used to make this over-the-tub wall arrangement for storage (below). The boxes may be any size to fit the area you have. Make them from ¾-inch exterior plywood, screwed and glued together. Use enamel paint to finish them to match your decorating scheme. Hang with angle irons and screws.

Chisel out a wall between the studs, and build
a shallow box from 1x3 or 1x4 pine lumber to fit
(above). The drop-down shelf is exterior-grade
plywood covered with plastic laminate. It is
hinged at the bottom with side braces.

This is a one-piece prefabricated shower unit
(right) that may be locked in place with fasteners
and adhesives. A good idea, if you have space,
is to plan a walled-in garden like this one. Window
glass is fixed in 2x6s, and double-glazed to shut
out weather. Floor is vinyl plastic.

This sauna (below) is factory-made; you assemble
it in the space you have. Most prefabbed saunas
have redwood panels, bench, and electric heater.
Note how ceramic tile was fitted into overall plan.
The sauna secret is to get a heater with enough
BTU output to heat the space; it should have a
thermostat so you can adjust it.

This wall-hung unit (below) utilizes exterior
plywood with A-A face (the best) on both sides.
It was finished with stain, although paint may be
used. If you use paint, buy inexpensive plywood.
The magazine shelf is removable, so flush tank
repairs can be made. Doors use semi-hidden
hinges; a saw slot is needed for mounting.

Bathroom Additions

Whether you're adding a small powder room or a full-sized bathroom to existing space or new construction, the key is to carefully plan for adequate space, water supply, and drainage.
The space you're hunting may be in the attic, basement, or master bedroom closet. Or it may be tucked under a stairway, hidden in a hallway, or even be in an attached garage.

Powder Room

Finding enough space for a powder room isn't difficult: it may be in a corner of a room, at the end of a hallway, or created by combining two closets. Keep the plan square; minimum space is about 4x4 feet for a lavatory and toilet. The big problems you'll face are water and drainage pipe connections, teamed with ventilation and sound conditioning.

If possible, locate the powder room as close as possible to existing plumbing lines. Most houses are built around a 'wet wall'—the wall up through which water supply and drainage pipes are threaded. Naturally, the closer to this wall you can get with any bathroom addition the better. It will save time and material expense in making new connections.

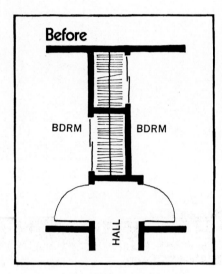

This small bathroom was created at the end of a hallway separating two bedrooms—a common plan. Two side-by-side closets were rearranged to accommodate the square plan. Only about a foot in width was lost in each bedroom. The ventilating fan exhausts in the attic, and the soil stack for the toilet runs up through the closet and out of the roof. Vinyl floor covering was carried up the wall as a decorative effect.

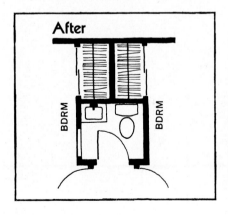

Because of moisture created by the tub/shower and lavatory, water-resistant materials and adequate ventilation are two important considerations for a small 'inside' bathroom. High-pressure laminate was specified here for cabinet fronts, wall wainscoting, soffits, and ceiling. The shower is tiled from the floor to the ceiling.

Relocating a closet created the space for this bathroom. Heating was tapped from bedroom duct; lighting was hooked into former closet wiring. Since bathroom is flanked by two bedrooms, sound-deadening wallboard was used over outside studs. Alternate plan could have doorway coming from one bedroom. Or plan could have two doorways: one from a bedroom; the other from hall.

Three-Fourths Bath

This is a plan variation of the powder room shown at the left. The closets in the bedroom were eliminated, creating the necessary space for a square shower unit. Minimum space for a three-fourths bath is about 4x8 feet, although you can purchase a mini-sized shower unit, reducing this by about one foot.

Include storage and fixtures in your basic plan. If space permits, provide storage with base and wall cabinets. If it doesn't, build shallow wall cabinets between the studs. And don't overlook the space above the shower stall, bathtub, and toilet for additional storage. However, be sure these units are made from water-resistant materials, or covered with them.

Fixtures are 'storage units', too. Consider installing medicine cabinets and recessed soap and tissue holders between studs so they don't stick out into the room, causing traffic problems.

In an 'inside' bathroom, ventilate with an exhaust fan or a skylight. For a skylight, build a 'light box' from ¾-inch plywood to go through an attic 'crawl space' area. However, if the bathroom is on an outside wall, use a window unit for light and ventilation; but be sure to locate it away from the bathing area to deter cold drafts.

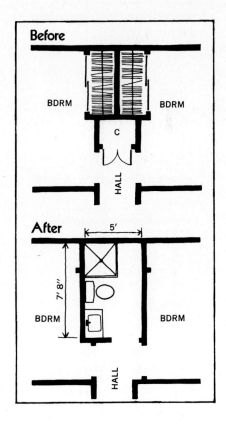

Use space-savers such as pocket and sliding doors, and don't be afraid to borrow space from adjoining rooms to expand a small bath. Chances are you can rearrange the room for extra space. This is especially true of large master bedrooms; make use of the extra footage. Let it spill over into the bathroom.

A full-bath version of the four-foot unit is possible if your bedroom closets are back-to-back. You can 'spread' the closets to accommodate a compact-mentalized bathroom, as was done below. Or remove the closets and relocate them for even more space. Minimum space is about 6x9 feet; anything over this is a bonus that may be utilized for luxury features.

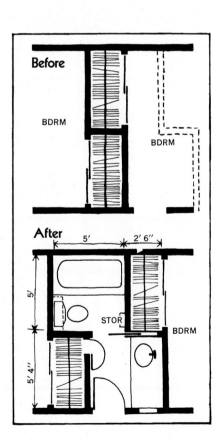

Full Bath

Because of the space required to add a full bathroom, you can incorporate many ingenious ideas into your plan. These may include a sunken tub in which to soak, a sauna, a dressing area, a steam room—even sunbathing and lounging areas.

If you include one or more of these niceties, take care to ensure that the facilities can be used by more than one member of the family at the same time. Accomplish this by dividing the area into compartments. Plan, too, for the future. Right now, your children may be small. But in a few years, they'll be old enough to appreciate the 'luxury' of an exercise room or sunbathing area.

Although space may limit you to something less than a Roman spa, there are materials and products available that stretch space and actually transform the 'traditional' bathroom into a 'rest and recreation room'. These include 1-piece molded tubs/showers; toilets that look similar to a dressing table bench; sliding doors that make compartments; special shapes of fixtures that take advantage of wasted corner space; fixtures that do double-duty, such as portable, flexible shower units; and combination lamps for heat/vanity/general lighting. All of these materials may be found at building supply outlets, home centers, and catalog stores.

Select the Right Materials

A bathroom *addition* is more complex than a bathroom remodeling. You'll probably have to add plumbing and make some structural changes to create the necessary space—even for a small powder room.

Generally, you will need a building permit for this work. You'll probably find, too, that certain plumbing and wiring codes will have to be met, according to local specifications. It's best to have a remodeler or builder do the work—he will take care of the permits. To keep the remodeling cost down, you usually can do the rough-in and finish carpenter work with standard hand tools.

Flooring materials: Your floors must be structurally sound to support the weight of bathroom fixtures. Although most homes are constructed to handle the extra load, be extra cautious if you're planning a second-story bathroom addition. The area you are considering using might not be supported by a partition wall below, or have joists that are strong enough to hold the weight without reinforcement.

One way to find out is to check the blueprint and specification sheets for your home. If you don't have these available, consult a builder for help in this area.

For any new material you select to install, floor preparation is standard. If the floor is carpeted, remove the old carpeting as well as the partition walls and fixtures. The finish floor underneath may be hardwood, resilient tile, or just a plywood subfloor. Generally, you can lay new materials over the old. But consult your building supply retailer who will give you recommendations on installation techniques for the floor you choose. Of course, no type of flooring should be installed until the addition is complete.

Ceramic tile is a good choice for bathroom flooring, as it is water- and moisture-proof. You have a wide range of colors from which to choose, along with different sizes.

It's absolutely essential that ceramic tile be laid over a sound surface; otherwise, the base eventually may loosen and pop the tile above it. The first step is to take the old flooring material right down to the bare subfloor. If the floor is hardwood, you don't have to pull it up. You should, however, make sure that the surface is smooth (rent a sander) and free from protruding nails.

Then, lay a waterproof building paper over the subfloor. Overlap it about three inches at the seams and about an inch up the walls. Now you can lay the tiles.

Tiles are sold in sheets with a paper backing—or 'fronting.' Spread waterproof mastic over the prepared subfloor, set the tiles, and tap lightly with a hammer, using a block of wood as a buffer. Let the tiles set for several days, then remove the paper and grout the joints with a mixture specially made for this.

Resilient tile and sheet flooring also work well in bathrooms. You can buy 9x9- and 12x12-inch squares in a countless number of colors and patterns. Sheet or strip flooring is manufactured in various widths, colors, and patterns. Some is even textured to simulate the "feel" of real brick and stone.

Proper floor preparation is the key to a professional-looking job; the floor has to be smooth, level, and dinner-plate clean. This is true regardless of the surface you are covering —old resilient flooring, hardwood, or subflooring of plywood or hardboard.

Carpeting and carpet tiles, available in a variety of colors, textures, and patterns, may be used in the bathroom, too. Just make certain that the carpeting you purchase is moisture resistant.

Prepare the subfloor the same way for carpeting as you would for any other material. Then install the carpeting, using double-sided tape. Apply the tape directly to the floor.

Hardwood strip flooring or blocks, although suitable for use in the bathroom, should be kept out of the shower/tub area because of moisture problems.

After preparing the subfloor, lay the hardwood strip flooring over waterproof building paper. The strips are tongue-and-grooved, so attaching them to the subfloor is easy. Simply nail through the tongues about every four to six inches. Since the wood is very tough, you may have to drill pilot holes for the nails. At the walls of the room, it's best to face-nail the flooring in place—you won't have room to swing a hammer for tongue nailing. Here, countersink the nails, and fill the holes with matching wood putty.

Hardwood blocks are similar to resilient tiles. Some have tongue-and-groove edges; others are simply laid in a bed of mastic or over double-coated adhesive tape made for this purpose. Most hardwood blocks are pre-finished. But you will have to finish hardwood strip flooring (some is prefinished) with pene-trating sealer and top coats.

Paint is not recommended for bathroom floors because of moisture.

Wall treatments: Whether you're moving closets to obtain space or building anew, par-tition walls are involved.

In old construction, you must make sure that the partition wall you plan to take out is not load-bearing. If it is load-bearing, taking it out will damage the house structurally un-less you devise a special support. As a rule, load-bearing walls run *across* the joists. There are, of course, some exceptions to this. If you are in doubt, be sure to check with a builder.

Existing walls also may contain heating ducts, wiring, and plumbing. Check this out, too, before you start ripping.

Partition walls usually consist of a 2x4 head-er and a plate with 2x4 studs sandwiched between. The wall surface probably will be gypsumboard or plaster.

To remove the wall, break through the covering and pry it off the studding. Then remove the studs, header, and plate. The ceil-ing and floor material probably butts against the header and plate, so this gap will have to be patched with gypsumboard.

By working carefully, you may be able to save some of the studs for re-use. However, if you need additional framing material, pur-chase No. 2 grade, blemish-free and straight. But, you may use metal studs for this.

Build the new wall just like the old one: toenail the studs to the header and plate, which are nailed to the ceiling and floor. Space the studs 16 inches on center. And be sure to install wiring and heating ducts before sur-facing the wall.

Gypsumboard wall panels should be at least 3/8 inch thick to cover the studs. For the inside walls of the bathroom use gypsumboard that is surfaced with a waterproof paper; for the outside walls substitute regular gypsum-board since moisture isn't a problem here.

Fasten the material to the studs with gyp-sumboard nails, staggering them about four inches apart. Drive the nails flush and then hit them one more time. This 'dimples' the gypsumboard just enough so the nails won't pop. Cover the nail heads with gypsumboard tape and/or cement. The joints of the boards are slightly tapered to accept the thickness of the tape, which adheres to the surface with the help of cement and a wide scraper.

Now, install finishing materials over the gypsumboard. If you use paneling or tile, you may not have to tape the gypsumboard joints behind the material.

Prefinished paneling can be used in the bathroom, but it shouldn't be exposed to running water, such as in a shower stall or as part of a backsplash.

You can apply paneling directly to the studs, but it is better to stick it over gypsumboard, using adhesive or nails.

For sound-conditioning, consider using sound-deadening board, insulation between the studs, or a double thickness of gypsum-board. Your building supply retailer will be able to provide you with the proper construc-tion techniques to reduce the decibel rating to an acceptable point.

Ceramic tile, either sheets with a paper backing or individual tiles, makes an excellent wall covering for bathrooms. Not only is it waterproof, it comes in a wide range of colors and sizes for floors, walls, and counter tops.

With the exception of a notched adhesive spreader, you do not need any special tools to install ceramic wall tile. You'll save a lot of cutting and trimming at corners and around fixtures if you apply the tile after the room has been properly laid out. Check with your building supply retailer for specific installation procedures and the proper adhesives.

Other wall coverings include plastic laminate, vinyl contact paper, regular wallpaper with a washable surface, and paint. If you want to mirror a wall, mirror squares are ideal. Install them as you would floor tile—but on the wall. For accents, consider simulated brick or stone. These products are resistant to moisture.

Bathroom fixtures: Premolded fiberglass tub/ shower combinations and regular porcelain products are available in a wide range of colors and shapes. Lavatories and toilets also fall into this broad product category. Your bathroom design will dictate the shapes and sizes that are necessary.

You can purchase bathtubs and showers prefabricated as well as in single units. The trick there is to have enough entry room to get the units into the space. If the units are especially large or odd-shaped, move them into position and connect them before you complete the framing of a partition wall. Cover the fixtures with paper or plastic so they won't be damaged during construction. Since local codes and plumbing skills are involved, hire a professional to connect the supply and drain lines to the tub/shower, lavatory, and toilet. The cost is not prohibitive.

Finding just the right lavatory for your bathroom won't be difficult. There are a great many to choose from: either freestanding units or those that can be built into cabinets. Preplan the location. If the lavatory is to be installed in a countertop, have the top prefabricated at a millwork shop. Some firms manufacture preformed countertops with a cutout for the lavatory. You simply lower it into the space and install the rim. You can even cover countertops with ceramic tile. Don't use linoleum.

For storage, either purchase prefabricated units that hang on studs, or build shallow cabinets between the studs. For special storage, you may want to build your own cabinets to fit unusual space. For this, use ¾-inch-thick exterior-grade plywood with an 'A' face and a 'C' or better back.

The plywood serves as a 'facing' material. It is nailed or screwed and glued to a framework of 2x4 members nailed to the studs. Doors can slide in an aluminum track you can buy; or you can hinge them. Use a penetrating sealer before you paint or stain the cabinets. They must be as moisture-resistant as possible.

Lighting and ventilation: These are the finishing touches on any bathroom addition. Start on them as soon as you've framed in the addition.

Lighting can be indirect via a suspended ceiling or direct with fixtures. Again, codes and your skill will determine whether or not you call in a professional to do this work. An electrician can rough-in the wiring and junction boxes; you probably can hook up the fixtures yourself.

Ventilate through a window, framed in along with the partition walls (doors, too). Or install an exhaust fan through an outside wall or the ceiling to get rid of smoke, odors, and so forth.

Where to get help: You can get design and building help from architects, builders, remodeling contractors, and building supply retailers. For materials, check your building supply outlet, general merchandise stores, plumbing contractor, furniture stores, and magazines devoted to building and remodeling.

Glossary

Grout—a fine, cement-like powder you mix with water to fill joints in ceramic tile. The right consistency is about like whipped butter. Grout may be colored; check dealer.

Load-bearing—refers to a partition wall that helps support a ceiling system. A load-bearing wall usually runs across the joists in the ceiling above it.

Resilient flooring—flooring materials such as asphalt, vinyl, vinyl-asbestos, cork, rubber, linoleum, and vinyl sheet. Sheet or strip type flooring usually is resilient.

Vapor barrier—is a material that will block the flow of moisture in walls to prevent condensation inside them. You can buy a membrane type barrier; it comes in rolls. Some paints offer a moisture barrier. The vapor barrier has to be part of the warm side of the wall or ceiling to be effective.

Ideas at a Glance

Finding the space for a new bathroom addition can be a problem, but only rarely is the problem insurmountable. Below, you'll find a floor plan of a fairly typical house. It may not be identical to your home's floor plan, but upon close examination, you should be able to spot similarities. The corresponding numbers show where a bathroom addition may be located with a minimum of structural construction. In your case, you may have to rearrange space to create enough room for the bath you want. You'll find two common bathroom arrangements: the square and rectangular type. Size, of course, depends on space.

1. *Floor space often is wasted in the closet area. By turning the closet to face the front door, you get space for a new bathroom. The entry space may have to be cut.*

2. *This plan utilizes space above the basement stairsteps. You usually can squeeze a couple of feet without loss of headroom below.*

3. *A middle-of-the-house location takes advantage of wasted hall space. Consider any hallway in the living area of your home, if there is an alternate traffic route. Here, it is through the kitchen area.*

4. *An attached garage often is overlooked for a bathroom addition. And, as a rule, there usually is enough space for a Roman spa-type bathroom, too. Plumbing hookups are easy; the floor can be elevated, if there are a couple of steps down into the garage. The area probably will have to be insulated to prevent freeze-ups in cold weather.*

5. *The space just inside a back entry is another good area—perhaps for a childrens' bath. Traffic is detoured a couple of steps through a breakfast room and informal dining area that is used just a few hours daily.*

6. *Most rooms in your home can yield several feet for a bathroom addition without losing any comfort. Here, a family room traded only five feet of length for a new bathroom, plus an extra closet. In planning, arrange the door so that the bathroom is hidden from direct view of adjoining rooms. The bath can serve both your family and guests.*

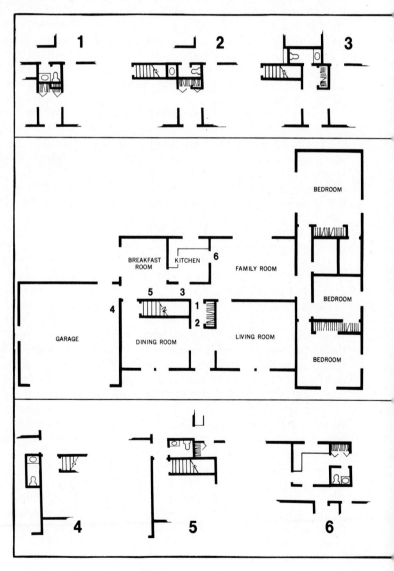

By rebuilding a master bedroom closet and taking seldom-used space, this bathroom could be built in a corner of a master bedroom. By building a partition wall, another lavatory could be added, too. Complete new water supply and drainage lines often are not necessary, if you can spot the bathroom on or near the 'wet wall' in your home. If space is limited, simply switch the bathtub unit for a shower stall combination. For extra storage space, the lavatory next to the toilet in this plan could be encased in a pre-fabricated cabinet unit. Compartments make this plan work well.

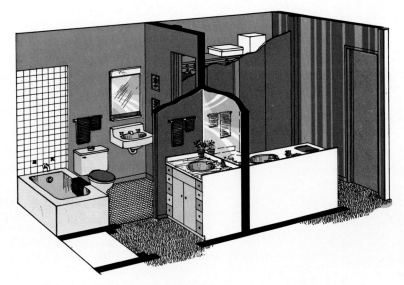

With either a remodeling or a brand-new addition, bathrooms can be made more functional in a bedroom area. In these examples, you can see how careful planning is the key to the clever use of often-wasted bedroom space. Sometimes, it is a matter of rearranging the furniture in the bedroom to create the extra space necessary for a bathroom. In an existing bathroom, the use of built-ins can add all the storage that you need. If the fixtures are old, switch them for new ones quickly and inexpensively. Often, you can do this yourself.

By realigning several fixtures, this bathroom now does the work of two. The bathtub in the old plan was turned 90 degrees so it butts against an outside wall. The compartment plan serves both the parents from an adjoining bedroom and the children from an off-the-hall lavatory location. Part of a closet was used to gain extra space; the closet is now even more usable since it has become a part of a lavatory/dressing room combination. Pocket-type doors add extra space to each compartment, while the closet is equipped with a folding-type door to help conserve space in the dressing area.

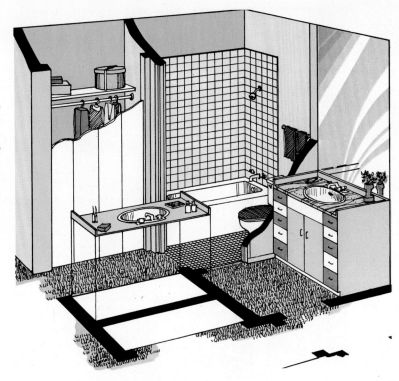

Garage Additions

A garage addition can be much more than a shelter for your car. You can gain extra storage and living space, and add architectural interest to your home. Whether you buy prefabricated components or build the garage from scratch, you'll find valuable design ideas and construction techniques in this section that will make the job easier.

Carport

A storage 'box' was built at the rear of the carport area with exterior plywood. It was framed in with 2x4s on 16-inch centers and skinned with the ¾-inch-thick material. One panel was left out of the rear wall for a doorway into the backyard area. The storage compartment has a front and rear door for access from either side. Floor of the carport is compacted gravel, which will serve as a base for a concrete floor.

This addition is nothing more than a roof extension that provides shelter for a car and storage for outdoor living supplies and lawn and garden equipment. Other than the tar-and-gravel built-up roof, the rest of the framing and finishing is a simple project for any handyman who has hand tools and some building skill.

The roof structure is supported by 2x6s doubled and spaced about ¾ inch apart. The 2x6s are fastened to square concrete piers set below frost line.

A panel of plywood separates the carport from the house structure and helps to create an enclosed entrance to the house. Another panel of the same material is used for a windbreaker on the outside of the carport. The rafters are 2x10s spaced on 24-inch centers, and the fascia is designed to perfectly match the fascia on the house, which ties in the carport architecturally.

Detached

Through smart planning and design, this detached garage addition can add a sheltered entrance to your home, a two-car garage, and a storage area for lawn and garden equipment. The clerestory on the garage roof could provide plenty of natural light for a workshop or laundry area in a corner.

To add more architectural interest and mass to the house, a small areaway was designed between the storage area and garage, so the homeowner doesn't have to walk around outside to reach it. If your home has a swimming pool, or if you're planning one, the storage area could be adapted into a cabana arrangement or a poolside serving area for refreshments.

The concrete driveway near the trees was widened about 10 feet to provide additional off-street car parking facilities for guests. A sunken well was built for the large trees. The well is encased by brick layed up in a random pattern with mortar.

By using similar building materials for roofing, siding, and trim pieces, this garage addition flows into the house design without breaking architectural lines. The height of the shed roof on the storage area is the same as the height of the garage roof. From the front, both structures visually appear as a single unit. Well-placed plantings also help frame the addition on the lot.

Attached garage is really an extension of your home. The roof framing is simple: a hook-on to the siding or roof. Sidewalls may be standard framing, too, with studs placed on 16- or 24-inch centers. Windows and doors have double headers; the garage door framing should be double members to support an overhead door. It's practical to insulate the space, using ridge or gable louvers for adequate ventilation. Reinforce the floor for car weight.

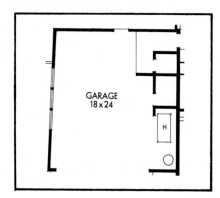

GARAGE
18 x 24

Attached Garage

One of the major features of an attached garage is that it may be heated for family activities during cool weather. You may pipe heat from the main house into the garage space or install an inexpensive heater. Part of the garage, then, may be designed into a workshop, laundry area, sewing center, or a playroom.

The key to adding an attached garage to your home is design: the addition should match or complement the architecture of your home; the same types of materials should be used. In this example, the garage roof matches the house roof at the peak; the same styles of siding and shingles were used, so the garage becomes an integral part of the house.

If the garage will be heated and used for family activities, it should be insulated. The framing can be quickly covered with gypsumboard for a more finished look. Be sure to provide a rear access door so lawn and garden equipment and outdoor furniture may be easily stored. An entry door into the house also should be provided. Windows and doors should match those used throughout the house for architectural unity.

Select the Right Materials

You can have the garage addition you want, if you have the space. Many building supply retailers have precut garages for sale. There also are garage 'specialty' dealers who will erect a garage for you; these firms offer several styles from which to choose. Or, you can build the garage yourself.

Floor treatments: If you go the route of home construction—and if you want to cut part of the cost of having the garage structure professionally installed—first build a base. Concrete is best. It's strong; impervious to decay; resists termites, rodents, and dampness; and, best of all, is relatively easy to put down—especially with ready-mix concrete. And, if your plans call for finishing part of the garage addition into more living or work space, it makes a good base or subfloor.

The size of the concrete floor depends on the size of your addition. Dimensions for a single-car garage range from 11x19 feet to 16x25 feet. Plan on at least 25x25 feet for a full double garage. Make it larger, if possible.

At the time of construction, a double garage won't cost twice as much to build as two single units. However, it is expensive to remodel a single garage into a double garage. So, plan your job for future needs.

Thickness of the slab and the footings required will depend on the codes in your area. Generally, the thickness runs between three and five inches. For added strength, reinforce the slab and the footings with steel rods and/or reinforcing mesh. Again, codes will specify the type of material you will need.

Grade preparation is very important before the concrete is placed. If the subgrade is not properly compacted, the slab may settle and crack. Be sure to remove all grass, sod, and roots. And, if there are soft spots in the ground, dig them out and fill them with sand, gravel, crushed stone, or slag.

Use granular fills of gravel, sand, and/or crushed stone to bring the grade to final level. Compact this material with a tamper (the fill should not be more than 4 inches thick). Extend the fill about a foot beyond the slab to prevent undercutting from rain, and for drainage.

Of the three major foundations, T-, slab, or piers, slab is the easiest to build. However, local codes may dictate your decision.

First waterproof slab foundations before placing the concrete by inserting a waterproof membrane between the slab and the ground. Polyfilm is especially good for this.

Order ready-mix concrete a week or so before you're ready to place the slab. The concrete company will help you estimate your needs. Simply tell them the length, width, and thickness of the slab. By ordering early, you may be able to take advantage of reduced rates.

Finishing concrete requires a helper or two. One person has to screed (level) the concrete while another shovels the mixture in holes and compacts the mixture. You may need a helper on the other end of the screed, too, if the job is big. Another friend can begin troweling the concrete while the rest of the work is being finished. Speed is important. If the concrete sets, you've got big problems. Plan the job so there's no waiting.

Next use side forms for the concrete to level the slab, which should be slightly pitched for drainage. You can use 2x4-inch lumber for a 4-inch slab; 2x6s are best for 5- and 6-inch slabs. Since 2x4s and 2x6s are not really 4 or 6 inches wide (1½x3½ inches for 2x4s), you'll have to elevate the forms slightly. Then, backfill outside the forms to prevent the concrete from spilling out from under them.

Use 1x2s, 2x2s, or 2x4s for stakes for the forms, and space them at about 2- to 3-foot intervals. Drive the stakes slightly below the top of the forms so the concrete surface is easier to finish with a screed and trowel.

Double-check your measurements and level before any concrete is placed.

Before edging the concrete, cut it away from the forms with a trowel. At this point, install sill bolts for the garage framing. Also insert any expansion strip material, according to the design of the garage. Always use expansion strips between other foundations and concrete work such as driveways, sidewalks, and patios. This will deter cracking.

Use a wooden float to smooth the concrete. Floating helps to embed large pieces of aggregate, remove imperfections in the surface, and compact the concrete. On large jobs, use knee boards to get out on the surface.

If you want a smooth surface, use a steel trowel to finish the concrete. Keep the trowel flat on the surface, and use wide sweeps and overlap the passes. Don't tip the trowel or the surface will be rippled.

Concrete must be cured to add strength and durability. Moisture-cure it by keeping the whole slab wet with wet coverings or by sprinkling it with a hose. Keep the surface wet for at least five days during hot weather and seven days in cooler weather (below 70 degrees).

Wall treatments: Garage addition framing is simple for a handyman to do. However, have a plan for the garage, since spacing of the framing members may depend on the weight of the roof structure *and* whether or not you plan to add a room above the garage.

If the garage will be used for car shelter and, perhaps, for a workshop or laundry center use 2x4-inch studs on 24-inch centers for the wall framing. If the garage will support rooms above the slab, have the studs on 16-inch centers—just like your home—or according to codes or your architect's plans.

Nail the 2x4s to the sill plates (bolt the slab to these) and double 2x4 headers at the roof line. Also double the corner studs and do any door and window framing when the walls are erected. Windows require double framing at the top, sides, and bottom; a garage door takes at least double 2x6s or 2x8s for the header with double 2x4s at the jambs or sides. If desired, you can buy prefabricated wall panels for the basic enclosure.

Construct any needed *partition walls* in the garage after the roof goes on.

Finishing materials include plywood or insulation board, sheathing covered with siding on the outside, and gypsumboard or paneling on the inside. If you are planning to finish the inside of the garage, install insulation (if needed) before fastening the finishing material to the studs. The vapor barrier faces inside.

Ceiling treatments: Frame the roof after the sidewalls are up—flat, pitched, hipped, to complement the architecture of your home.

If the roof will be shingled, and the pitch isn't too great, you may be able to do this job yourself. But hire a professional if the roof is a built-up tar-and-gravel structure, or if the roof is highly pitched. In this case, scaffolding is generally required for safety.

Framing members are usually 2x6s for rafters. Or, purchase prefabricated roof trusses. These are easier to install than cutting notches and fitting standard rafter framing. Spacing of the rafters usually is 16 inches on center; this varies, depending on the snow and wind loads in your area. Local codes will specify the structural roof design.

The garage ceiling may be left open, or you may cover it with ceiling tile, gypsumboard, or plastic panels. Tack in insulation before installing the ceiling materials—especially if the garage will be used and heated for additional work or living space.

Details and appointments: In most areas a building permit is needed for a garage addition. This may be obtained from the city building department. To qualify for the permit you will probably have to have a plan of the addition—professionally done or a rough sketch. A quick way to check this is to ask your local building material retailer or phone the city building department.

Determine your lot line before you start any building. The addition, of course, has to be within your lot line.

Design the garage addition so it becomes a part of the overall architectural design of your home. It should not look as if it has been stuck on your lot or built as an afterthought.

Plan around the addition. If the garage will be attached, consider adding a patio, breezeway, or porch. If the garage will be detached from the house, you may want a covered walkway between the two for weather protection.

Don't overlook landscaping around the garage addition either. Plan on a driveway that's wide enough to accommodate off-street parking for guests.

Lighting for a regular garage addition is minimum. It should be on a separate circuit that runs from your main electrical house entry. Bury the wires.

Provide power for an exterior light at the front and rear of the garage, and at least one light inside the garage. Connect all of these from a three-way switch that is operated from inside the garage, inside the house, and on the walkway. Use single switches for separate lights within the garage.

If a workshop or a laundry center is in your plans, wire the garage for power tools and appliances. Have at least a 220-volt line into the garage for these work areas. If you will use part of the garage for a living area, install wiring and plumbing when you're constructing the addition. This can save money.

The number of windows and doors you'll need depends on the use of the garage and its design. For a car shelter only, you won't need fancy windows; they should match the rest of the architecture of your home, however. Garage doors may be overhead, single swing-out, or double swing-out. You can even buy an overhead door with an electronic opener/closer. The cost is not prohibitive. You'll also need a standard entrance door (you can buy them prehung—as window units) and another door for entry to lawn and garden storage. Use extra wide doors here.

Ventilation is especially important if you are going to use your garage addition for extra living or work space. For a car shelter, provide ventilation with small aluminum, wooden, or screen wire louvers inserted into the gable ends of the garage. To ventilate the addition, use a strip of louvers for the ridge of the roof.

Where to get help: Architects, builders, remodelers, or specialists in garage construction will be able to help you with your garage addition. Ask for standard plans first.

If you plan to do a lot of the work yourself (such as place the concrete slab), consult an architect, builder, or concrete contractor for the exact specifications. For references, call your local contractors' association. And don't

overlook local landscaping architects and contractors for special help.

Your best sources for materials are building material outlets, ready-mix concrete firms, and specialty stores. Also, visit your library and newsstand for books and magazines.

Plan your job: Codes and building permits almost dictate garage addition planning. Ask the city what requirements are necessary to obtain a permit. The answer to this question will determine to what extent plans will have to be drawn for your specific lot.

Stick to modules—4-foot increments—in design. All building materials are manufactured on a 4-foot dimension.

Plan space. A car takes about 9x20 feet of space. Consider, too, lawn and garden storage; work areas; living areas; and play areas. The ceiling of the garage, for example, may be planned so that you can install an indoor basketball practice hoop for the kids.

Glossary

Backfill—To add dirt or other loose material against a concrete form or against the foundation wall of a house.

Cant strip—is usually a wedge-shaped piece of lumber that is used at the gable ends of a roof under the shingles or at the junction of the house and a flat deck under the roofing material. Used often in remodeling.

Course—a single layer of bricks, blocks, or shingles in the width of the material.

Float—to smooth the surface of fresh concrete. A wooden-like trowel is generally used for this. Floating works in large bits of aggregate. The next finish step is to steel trowel or brush the concrete surface.

Gable vents—are wooden or metal louvers installed at gable ends at the peak of the roof for ventilation within the structure.

Lookout—is a short bracket or cantilever, usually wooden, to support a roof overhang. This may be part of a rafter.

Module—generally a building measurement in a 2- or 4-foot increment. By designing in modules, you can save on material costs since materials are in modules. No special cutting or fitting may be needed.

Ideas at a Glance

For a handyman, garage additions offer an easy construction challenge, since components such as roof trusses, wall panels, and laminated structural beams can be used to frame in the addition. The job becomes one of assembly—like putting together a giant Erector Set—rather than fitting bits and pieces. The additions shown here all use components.

Exposed roof trusses form a garden area between this house and garage. The same trusses with the same support framing were carried into the garage where the trusses and framing were sheathed, roofed, and sided.

The floor is concrete with circles of exposed aggregate. Structural plastic sheets were fastened onto trusses in garden area; sidewalls have glass panels.

Vaulted roof supported by laminated beams adds architectural interest to this detached garage addition. It also provides a breezeway/entrance for the house and extra parking space.

Beams also visually carry the roof line of the house across the breezeway/carport to the garage. The driveway was doubled in width for the second car and for added parking facilities for guests.

Exposed framing at the corners and roof line of this double garage addition fits the architectural design of house. Added feature is parking facility at the side of the garage. Space otherwise would have been wasted. It also provides a turnaround for the cars parked in the garage and parking for guests.

Square patio blocks on a sand and gravel base create a walkway beside the asphalt-topped driveway.

Wide overhang on the garage matches the house overhang and provides a covered entrance into the house.

If you have plenty of space, this double parking space arrangement on both sides of a garage addition may be your answer to off-street parking for guests. The surfaced area also provides a play yard for small children. It is pitched slightly for adequate water drainage.

Landscaping helps soften the corners of the addition, which is tied into the side of the house. The wide overhang offers weather protection at the entrance to the home. Note how the garage gable matches the gable on the roof of the house for architectural alignment.

Patio Additions

A patio or deck is a fast, inexpensive, and imaginative way to add more space and architectural flair to your home. Both can be a solution for problem lots, the need for outdoor living space, or landscaping. Best yet, an average handyman can build a patio or deck with a few hand tools and some knowledge of the necessary construction techniques.

Off-Grade

From the turn of the century to the mid-1930s, most homes were built on high foundations. The front and back entrances were accessible via steps to a porch, or just steps leading to the door. If your home falls into this classification, you can adapt it to today's outdoor living by simply adding an off-grade deck and a sliding glass door or regular door for access. If the entrance is on-grade, but the lot falls away from the house on a sharp slope, a deck that is cantilevered over the slope is your best bet. It will allow you to take advantage of otherwise wasted space. A cantilevered deck must have adequate bearing support via concrete footings.

There are no set standards for deck sizes—except that they should be tailored to meet your entertainment requirements: do you usually host 10 or 50 persons? Your answer will dictate the size of the deck. The shape should conform with the design of your home—square, rectangular, or free-form.

This redwood deck is cantilevered over a sloping lot. Sliding doors were added for access from the dining room. The rear entry door was maintained for normal traffic up stairsteps at right. Double 2x10 joists support the columns, which are simply sandwiched between the joists and fastened with lag bolts. Alongside the house, the joists are toenailed to a 2x10 ledger strip that is fastened to the side of the house. Joist hangers also could be used here.

Grade-Level

Use either concrete or wood for grade-level patios and decks. The advantage of using concrete is that it holds up very well under weather conditions. One asset of a wood deck is that you may enlarge it easier than you could its concrete counterpart.

The deck above was built from garden-grade redwood, although cypress or specially treated fir could have been substituted. The framework is a rectangular box of 2x12s, with 2x12 'joists' on 24-inch centers supporting the flooring. The framework sits on concrete piers, below the frost line—usually 44 inches deep, unless you live in a very warm climate. Joist hangers were used on the horizontal 2x12s. The deck is freestanding; it is not attached to the house.

If concrete is your choice, you'll need to form its shape with either 2x4 or 2x6 lumber. Stake the forms solidly so the fresh concrete won't buckle them. You'll need a ½-inch asphalt expansion strip between the patio and the foundation of the house. This permits expansion and contraction without damage.

The design of this deck, in back of a typical tract house, lends itself to expansion. Redwood was used here since it won't rot from moisture. With redwood, you don't need stain or any protective coating. As a finishing touch, redwood chips were spread around the perimeter of the deck to seal off the underside of it. The chips are bordered with a frame of 2x4s to prevent chips from spreading. Only a handsaw, square, level, and hammer, plus fasteners, were used for the deck's fabrication.

If a tree is in the way of your deck planning, don't cut the tree down—go around it instead, leaving at least a four-inch gap around the trunk of the tree for growth. Skirting, as used here, gives the mid-level deck a finished look. Be sure to cover the earth under the deck with black polyethylene film to deter plant growth. Or use about two inches of gravel, if you wish. If the ground slope is not enough to move water away from the foundation of the house, you can achieve proper drainage under the decking with clay tile.

Mid-Level

This large deck substantially increased the living area of this house. It was built over sloping ground and encompasses a tree. The kitchen opens off the niche indented into the back of the house, making serving easier. The same back entry was used, so the sidewalls of the house didn't have to be changed.

Redwood lumber was used to fabricate the deck, with redwood boards as skirting around the perimeter. The railing is wrought iron, lag-bolted to the floor of the deck. For privacy, plantings surround the deck. At night, the walkways and the trees are lighted, producing a dramatic effect.

The floor is 2x10-inch redwood lumber laid flat across 2x12-inch joists, spaced 24 inches on center. This produces a planking effect, which is carried down the steps leading to the backyard.

To carry out the design, 3x6-foot exposed aggregate blocks were placed on-grade off the steps to the deck. The space between the blocks is filled with peagravel to keep weeds and grass at bay.

Select the Right Materials

Concrete, wood, brick, and precast concrete are all suitable for patio or deck construction. But steer clear of asphalt for a surface, as it tends to become soft and sticky when the temperature soars.

Patio surfaces: Concrete is the least expensive material to use. Since it is 'fluid' when placed, designs are only limited to the forming, which can be square, rectangular, or free-form.

Almost without exception, it's best to order concrete from a ready-mix company. It is cheaper, in the long run, than attempting to mix the concrete yourself. The exceptions might be if the job is a small one, or your home is located on a lot where a concrete truck can't back into the proposed patio site. Be sure you check widths between adjoining homes, fences, and other obstructions; you'll need about 12 feet clearance. Telephone and electric wires can be disconnected by the utility companies to accommodate the height of the truck. Call the utilities as to date.

If you prepare the grade properly, you shouldn't have any trouble laying a professional-looking concrete patio.

First, lay out the design. If you want a square or rectangular patio, use 2x4 or 2x6 lumber for forms, coating the inside of the forms with a special, prepackaged mixture that prevents concrete from sticking to the forms. Stake the forms about every two feet with 2x2-inch or 2x4-inch stakes driven solidly into the earth. Nail these stakes from the outside into the form with scaffolding nails (double-headed). This should hold the forming rigid and in position. Make sure that all forms are level, with a very slight pitch away from the house. If the forms are loose or weak, the thrust of the concrete can buckle them, causing a wavy edge.

If your plans call for a free-form patio, form the curves with a ¼-inch-thick tempered hardboard, cut to the proper width. The curves have to be rigidly staked. And be sure to nail through the hardboard into the stakes because hardboard is grainless and will not hold nails.

Prepare the ground by removing grass and other plant growth. You may have to excavate some areas so that the soil is level throughout the patio area.

Inside the formwork, use bricks (broken), stones, or gravel as a base for the concrete. Tamp these materials tightly and cover them with a base of sand. Wet the sand with a garden hose, then let the sand settle. This makes a firmer base for the concrete.

Ready-mix companies sell concrete by the cubic yard—27 cubic feet. To determine the amount of concrete you will need, figure the number of square feet in the area. For example, a patio slab 11 feet wide, 41 feet long, and four inches thick is 451 square feet. You multiply 11 by 41. Now divide this figure by three, since the slab is four inches thick—or 1/3 of a foot. This is 150 cubic feet. Divide this figure by 27 to determine the cubic yards. The answer is 5.55 cubic yards of concrete.

Other variables that will affect the price you pay for concrete include the day you want it delivered (some days are more costly than others, depending on schedules), unloading time, and the type of mix you want. Always have everything ready before the truck arrives; otherwise, you'll pay extra for the truck driver's time.

If you want decorative forms within the patio, use 2x4 or 1x4 redwood or cypress set on edge. Cover the wood with a sealer, then nail the pieces together with galvanized—not aluminum—nails.

You may tie the patio into the foundation of the house or leave it 'floating.' If you tie it into the foundation, use No. 5 reinforcing rods anchored into the foundation. You will have to drill holes for the rods. Then cement the rods into position with epoxy cement.

Reinforce the patio itself with steel mesh or reinforcing rods. This will help prevent cracking, which is caused by expansion and contraction from hot and cold weather.

When the concrete is placed, 'puddle' it with a spade to work out the air bubbles. Then 'screed' it (level the top) with a straight edge of 2x4 lumber. You'll need a helper for this. When the concrete starts to harden, trowel it to the finish you want. For a rough finish, use a wooden float. Or, for a brushed finish, use an old broom, sweeping the top surface lightly when the concrete is nearly set. However, you must trowel it fairly smooth first with a wooden float or it may be bumpy.

In hot weather, wet down the soil and base thoroughly with water before ordering the concrete. After the concrete has hardened overnight, keep it wet with water for a week or so to ensure a hard surface.

If the patio butts against the foundation of the house and if 'floating,' insert a ½-inch asphalt expansion strip between the foundation and the patio to guard against cracking. If the patio is in one piece, score the surface in about four-foot 'squares' with an edging tool to prevent the concrete from heaving.

For exposed aggregate sections, place the concrete, let it harden slightly, and cover the concrete with stones you can buy especially for this. Press the stones into the concrete with a flat edge of a 1x4, leveling from the surface of the forms. When the concrete is nearly dry, expose the aggregate by going over the concrete with a stiff-bristled push broom. Don't apply a lot of pressure to the broom, or it will dislodge the aggregate.

For patio blocks with exposed aggregate, first build the forms—unless you buy the blocks pre-cast. Use 2x4s for this, butt-joined and firmly nailed in squares or rectangles. Place the form on a smooth surface. Then fill it with a mixture of one part cement, two parts sand, and two parts pea gravel.

Tightly tamp this moistened material into your form, and level it. (The mixture should be about ½ inch below the top of the form.) Then spread the aggregate evenly over the surface. Press the aggregate into the concrete with a wooden float. When the concrete has hardened sufficiently to hold its shape, remove the form and let the block dry. If you'd rather have some freeform blocks, repeat the above procedure, using ¼-inch tempered type hardboard for the concrete form material.

Bricks are set on a sand base, the same as most patio blocks. Use paving bricks, or buy regular bricks and set them on edge. It's very important that the surface be level and lightly formed at the sides to maintain the shape you want. Lay down a sheet of black polyethylene film over the earth to deter plant growth. Then lay in the sand—a couple of inches—and level it. Next, set the bricks (or blocks) over the sand, and tap them with a hammer handle so they are firm. Then fill the cracks with sand, and water down the job with a garden hose. The sand will sink, so keep filling the cracks and watering them until they are full of sand. Use a broom to sweep in the sand. You may have to do this for several days.

Wooden decks: For these the best material to use is redwood, followed by cypress. The cost, however, may be prohibitive on your budget. If so, you may use specially treated fir.

As with all patios and decks, preplanning the design is the key to success. Use grid paper to lay out your job, taking into consideration trees, large shrubs, and the slope of the ground over which the deck will be constructed.

Because decks are structural and have to support weight, you should use 2-inch-thick lumber. The framing may be fastened to the house with nails or lag screws, or you can use metal joist hangers, which are fastened directly to the sill or foundation of the house. Make sure these supports are tied to the house framing—not just the siding or sheathing.

Support the deck every six feet or so away from the house—and at the corners—with concrete piers. For these, dig holes in the ground below the frost line, and fill them with concrete. Reinforcing rods make the piers even more solid, although you may not necessarily need rod. The piers should be at least one foot in diameter for adequate support. Again, this depends on the size of the deck and the amount of weight the piers must hold. Check your building supply retailer on this.

Because the lumber you use for decks is thick, simply butt-join the pieces together, using nails or lag bolts. And use 4x4-inch posts or double 2x4s for the columns from the top of the piers to the bottom of the decking. Joists across the deck should be 24-inches on center. If you anticipate a lot of weight on the deck, place the joists 16-inches on center for more support. The superstructure should be adequate for the weight to be placed on it.

For the decking, lay 2x4s or wider material flat across the joists and face-nail them into the joists with aluminum nails. Space the 2x4s about ¼ inch apart for adequate drainage. Don't butt the decking tightly together.

Accessories: You can build items such as benches and tables out of the same materials you used for the deck. Framing is simple; use butt-joints and metal L and U brackets for connections. Or, you may want to use galvanized plumbing pipe for legs. Screw the pipe into metal flanges that are screwed to the bottom face of either benches or tables.

If you want wrought iron railings, they're available at any building supply outlet. The sections are prefrabricated; you simply lagbolt or screw them into the decking material.

You can even fabricate patio or deck roofs from 1x4 louvers or structural plastic sheets. The sheets are made in 4x8-foot (smaller and larger) sizes—like plywood.

For corner posts for the roof use 4x4-inch lumber; attach the roof to the house with a ledger strip nailed to the studs of the house. Or make the roof freestanding.

If you use louvers, set them on edge and toenail them to joists running out from the house on four-foot centers. Use a 4x6-inch beam opposite the ledger strip to accept the weight of the joists at the end.

For plastic sheets, the framing is similar, but you should have a slight pitch away from the house for water drainage. Lighter framing material will work for the plastic sheets, since weight is not a factor. But allow for snow loads.

Prefabricated roofs and screened sidewalls are available for patios and decks. They usually are manufactured from aluminum; you simply bolt them into position, according to instructions furnished in the kit.

Where to get help: If you're unsure of what you want or don't know how to build a patio or deck, ask a professional for help. Even if you plan to do the work yourself, you still may want to consult an architect for design help. Your best source for having a patio or deck professionally built is a remodeler or builder. And the best time to contact these pros is in early spring or late fall, when their home building business is low.

Your building material retailer is another good source for planning and help with selection of building materials. And many magazines have special articles on planning and building patios and decks.

Planning: Building a patio or deck is not a difficult project. But don't let the simplicity fool you. The job should be thoroughly planned on paper before you start. Too, you may need to obtain a building permit from the city or your homeowner's association.

Since most wood materials will be exposed, make arrangements with your building material retailer to get the 'pick of the pile.' Every piece of lumber may not be perfect, but you may get a break. Concrete dealers will help you with estimates, mix, and delivery schedules.

Glossary

Aggregate—inert minerals such as sand, gravel, and crushed stone. There are two sizes: "fine", which is always sand, and "coarse"— usually crushed stone and gravel. Small, uncrushed stones may be used for exposed aggregate projects such as patio blocks.

Epoxy cement—a recent product on the market, it has three parts: cement, an emulsion, and hardener. You mix the latter two, then mix in the cement to the right consistency. It forms a very strong, quick-hardening bond.

Expansion strips—are bituminous board-like strips that are used to separate concrete and concrete blocks. The strips 'give' to prevent the concrete from cracking due to expansion and contraction from heat/cold.

Lag bolts—large, screw-like fasteners usually with square heads you turn with a wrench.

Puddling—to 'stir' fresh concrete with a shovel or mechanical vibrating device to work out air bubbles and voids in the mixture.

Screeding—leveling freshly placed concrete by running a straight-edge of a board across the tops of forms in a 'sawing' motion.

Ideas at a Glance

Benches, tables, shelter, and plantings combine to make your patio or deck more functional and livable. Although you can buy outdoor furniture, 'built-ins' help to carry out the overall design and may be fabricated from the same types of materials you used to construct the patio or deck.

Benches, tables, and shelter should be carefully planned to conform with the overall design of your patio or deck. In addition, they should match the architecture of your home.

Upright 4x4-inch posts, set into concrete at a slight angle, provide the main support for this perimeter bench. Seat supports are short 2x4s bolted to the posts. The seat back is 1-inch redwood lumber; the seat is 2x6s set about ¾-inch apart.

Legs of this bench are 4x4s set in concrete. The seat is 2x4s, bolted together and to the posts. A series of 1x4x6 spacers were used to separate the 2x4s. The terrace features a combination of natural concrete and aggregate. Design leads eyes to benches and plantings.

This sunken terrace utilizes a double deck to take advantage of the sloping ground. Retaining wall is capped with quarry tile; decking is redwood 2x4s spaced about ¼ inch apart; and the steps are the same material built the same way. Bottom of the terrace is concrete.

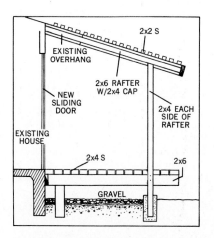

Patios and decks don't have to be assigned to the backyard. Front and side yards may be ideal, too. This deck-entrance adds interest and provides comfortable lounging.

This deck was elevated to height of entrance door with 4x4-inch posts encased in concrete. The rafters were hooked to the existing overhang; they are supported by double 2x4s on each side of the rafters. A 2x2 louver roof filters in the sunlight. Gravel under deck adds interest and stops plant growth.

Alternating 4x4-foot squares of redwood 2x4s are fastened to a frame of 2x4s and set on the ground, a concrete slab, or piers. You can build the sections yourself, or you may purchase them already built.

This brick patio utilizes a shelter constructed with a corrugated plastic roof. For support, 4x4-inch redwood posts were used, along with a 2x10 fascia. The roof is pitched slightly for drainage. Since shelter is fairly open, hanging plants may be used. Back of shelter is fabricated with 4x8-foot sheets of exterior-grade plywood. Storage area was built at left.

Basement Conversion

Stuck for more space in your home? Turn to the basement. Instead of using that space for off-season storage of worn-out clothing, old snow tires, and lawn and garden equipment, partition it as a laundry center, a family game room, and a workshop. This area provides more remodeling space for less money than any other in the home.

Family Room

Changing that unused space in the basement into an attractive family room is easy if you throw caution to the wind and think big! Use all the space. A bar in the corner, storage shelves along the walls, a window wall complete with dropped patio and plants, a central free-standing fireplace, or a game room with a pool table or table tennis—all are ideas you can incorporate in the dingy room under the first floor.

Look to the floors, walls, and ceiling. If any of these areas need repair, do this first. A daub of paint, some Sheetrock, and a throw rug often are all that is needed to give life to the room.

For information on fitting your basement family room, turn to the Select the Right Materials section; you'll find other ideas starting on page 55.

With a minimum of work and money, the bleak, bare billiard room above became a vibrant game room.

First, the wide-spreading overhead lamp was replaced with a light that cast its light where it was needed, and then a make-believe skylight was installed. To achieve this the blocking between the floor joists and the siding on the exterior of the house were removed for the small panels, and acrylic plastic panes were inserted into frames made of 2x2s and attached at the end of the joists. The sand-textured gypsumboard attached to the walls on 2x2 furring strips heightens the effect of the sunlight. Helping to maintain the illusion of a skylight is the gypsumboard panels at a 45-degree angle between the ceiling and the wall trim. The trim is made of 1x6s set on 2x2 furring strips. The same for the baseboard.

Lastly, a plywood cabinet was built below the end window, and indoor-outdoor carpet was laid.

This handyman's delight (left) started out as a drab area (below). Subflooring, dropped ceiling, pegboard, fluorescent light, and a workbench were all that was necessary to turn the area into one that even the most hammer-banged handyman could enjoy.

First, 2x4 sleepers were laid on the concrete and covered with a subfloor of hardboard. Tongue-and-groove wood tiles were laid on top.

Then, acoustical tile was stapled to 1x2-inch furring strips that run at right angles to the first floor. As a precaution, insulation was packed between the tile ceiling and the floor above.

Because of its versatility as a rack for many tools, pegboard was used from floor to ceiling on both walls of the workshop atop a layer of sheet plastic stapled to studs on 24-inch centers.

Lastly, a long fluorescent light was installed directly over the workbench, plus small spotlight fixtures where power equipment normally is used. Paint odors, dirt, and sawdust are eliminated with an electronic filter attached to the furnace blower. As an alternate, a ventilating exhaust fan could be used.

Shop Area

There's nothing difficult to fitting a workshop in your basement, even if you have only a small corner. With the addition of pegboard, drawers, cabinets, and workbench, you have all you'll need for all but the most elaborate project. But plan your remodeling carefully so that every tool has its place and yet is handy to reach when a specific job calls for it.

Before you move in that power tool equipment you've had your eye on for some while, make sure that you have an entrance to the basement large enough to take out your projects, and more than an 8-foot ceiling height—to stand up standard sheets of plywood. And build your workshop by a 220-volt outlet.

Besides these basic cautions, don't place your workshop inside-the-home beneath the living room. A sander below will wreck conversation above. And keep the shop away from the heating plant.

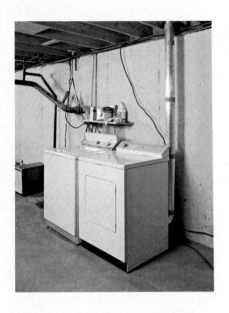

Laundry Center

Somebody has to do the laundry, but it needn't be a backbreaking chore. Dispel the gloomy Monday feeling with a center that is bright, bold, and filled with color. And plan the center so that everything you need is close-at-hand.

Install cabinets above the washer/dryer. Washing ingredients then will be ready when you need them and can be hidden when not in use.

Build a workbench close by the dryer. Clothes flow easily from the bench to the washer/dryer, then back to the bench for folding—and possibly ironing.

Make sure that there is plenty of light. Recessed lighting or fluorescent tubes over the area make washday more pleasant. And lay down carpet that is color-coordinated to the area's decorating scheme. You must do the laundry, so make the center a place you enjoy.

The tangled mass of wires and length of exposed pipe made this laundry center (above) as inviting as the Monday morning blues. But some structural alterations and general remodeling turned the area into one anybody would enjoy working in.

Like any other conversion, this new laundry center (below) had to be carefully planned to organize as much workable space as possible into a minimum configuration. This project has the further advantage of freeing the rest of the basement.

First, the exposed pipes and wires were hidden behind a gypsumboard wall that also set off the area from the rest of the basement. The board was set on 2x2s.

Then, new lights and a bright indoor-outdoor carpet were installed, and a workbench was built. You can easily move the wash from the washer/dryer to the bench.

Lastly, a supply cabinet above the washer and dryer and one above the workbench were built in.

With such a well-designed, color-coordinated laundry center, Monday wash is a joy.

Select the Right Materials

The key word here is below-grade. Or to put it in layman's language, below ground level. As any area below the level of the ground is prey to water seepage, you'll need materials that specify below-grade. Whether it's paint, tile, board, carpet, paneling, or any other general surface covering, if you're not sure about its use in a below-grade area, ask the supplier for some help.

Floor coverings: Before you paint, lay tile or wood parquet, or roll out carpet on your floor, decide what treatment the floor will receive. If you are building a workshop, don't use shag carpet. Keeping it clean would be an enormous chore. And wood parquet would stain the first time you spill on it. So, in a work area, select a material—carpet, tile, wood, or paint—that you can keep clean and one that won't stain.

Note the condition of the floor, especially if you want a finished floor. In older homes you'll often find cracked floors or evidence of water seepage. If so, first repair the concrete flooring. Otherwise, you might have to redo all your work just when you are getting used to it.

Carpet: Although one of the most common aboveground coverings, carpet is best left out of the basement—unless it is approved by the manufacturer for below-grade use, or if you install a built-in floor, then lay the carpet on top.

One exception to this general rule is indoor-outdoor carpet, which works well in most areas of the basement. It is comfortable underfoot and does not take too much maintenance. Make sure the basement will remain dry, and use a waterproof glue. For best results, follow the manufacturer's recommendations.

Tile: A natural for basements, tile is available in easy-to-work-with 9x9-inch or 12x12-inch squares, or in roll or sheet form. Available in a variety of patterns and colors, tiles are suitable for use in all basement areas.

Before you lay the tile, make sure the concrete floor is clean—free from general dirt, grease, and old paint. Scrub it first with muriatic acid and warm water. Let it dry completely.

Then lay your tile. To install, coat the concrete with a waterproof adhesive and lay the tile over it. Some tile has adhesive as part of the package. You peel off the backing and stick the tile onto the floor.

Wood: Another popular floor covering, wood works well only on top of a subfloor. Available in parquet blocks, tiles, or strips with tongue-and-groove edges for easy locking, it is fairly simple to install. Lay sleepers on the concrete, and use shims to level the floor. Then, lay the wood flooring on a subfloor of hardboard or plywood, as wood flooring will warp if proper installation recommendations are not followed, or if the basement is not dry. If you have any misgivings about how to install your basement flooring, write to the National Oak Flooring Manufacturers Association, 814 Sterick Building, Memphis 3, Tennessee, for instruction booklets.

Paint: The least expensive type of floor covering, paint is decorative and easy to apply. But, it is not comfortable underfoot. So, don't use it unless you prefer decoration to comfort.

Be sure to use a good grade of paint—one designed for use on concrete. But first, fill in any cracks, then remove all old paint and clean the floor of grease. Again, use muriatic acid and warm water.

Wall coverings: Not so long ago, there weren't options available for basement 'face-lifting.' Today, there is a wide variety—paneling, Sheetrock, paint, shingles, vinyl, plaster, and tapestry.

Use common sense when choosing the surface material. Don't Sheetrock a wall if there is a chance of penetration by sharp objects, or waste money paneling a workshop—you'll cover up most of the paneling. And don't use materials that are susceptible to mildew or mold. They can rust metal tools.

First, rid the walls of moisture. A coat of waterproof paint usually will do the trick. If not, patch the walls.

Paneling: For dressing up a dreary basement, there's nothing quite like paneling—natural wood, hardboard, or plastic laminate. But, because of its high cost, you may have to reserve wall paneling for a family room.

Moisture is about the only problem, and this can be corrected easily by preparing the walls properly. Develop a vapor barrier (to avoid moisture) by first installing studs on 24-inch centers, using fiber anchor plugs, flange-type screw anchors, lead anchors, adhesives, or concrete nails, then by laying sheet plastic over the strips and stapling. Put up the paneling, using adhesive fasteners or small nails to fasten it to the framing.

Sheetrock: This is an inexpensive basement wall material. But difficult to install for you must finish all joints that abut. For a clean, smooth result use perforated tape and plaster. Because it is tricky to join as a standard 4x8 sheet of Sheetrock, it's best to consult someone who has done this work before.

Paint: If your budget is tight, but you still want to do something to add color to the basement, try paint. Be sure to use below-grade paint and one that is suitable for the material it will be applied to. To ensure good results, talk to your paint dealer.

Miscellaneous: If you are looking for a special look for your basement walls, try using cedar shake shingles applied to a furred-out wall of plywood. These rough shingles add textural beauty to the most dingy area. Or drop a tapestry or some fabric from the ceiling to the floor. This produces a rich effect in a room where you don't want to attach materials to the walls. Be careful that the fabric is out enough from the wall that no water damage is possible. Do this even *after* you have taken care of the water damage.

Ceilings: Installing a ceiling in your basement goes a long way toward giving the area a 'finished' look. In addition, the ceiling can provide soundproofing to deaden the voices of children in the game room or the steady hum of a drill or saw in the workshop. And you can add fireproofing.

Make the ceiling high enough so that a short, sharp jab with a cue stick will not puncture a panel, and so that the workshop is not too low to allow easy movement of materials. In general, a workshop height of nine feet is minimum. For an overall finished look, drop the ceiling and enclose ducts and pipes. But plan so that there is enough headroom when the work has been completed.

Acoustical ceiling: These fiber noise-gatherers come in a wide range of finishes—pebbles, swirls, warm neutral colors, and metallic accents—that add decorative beauty to a ceiling, and are easy to install. Staple the tiles to the joists, or run 1x2-inch furring strips at right angles to the joists and staple the tiles to the furring strips.

For a suspended grid system, pre-made runners are available. These attach to the wall and the upper floor joists. For installation, check the manufacturer's instructions. When the grid system is in place, slip the light panels through the opening and lay onto the runners, leaving out one section for installation of a light panel or trougher.

Sheetrock: Although it is easy to decorate and easy to apply to existing floor joists—or around pipes and ducts—Sheetrock is not always recommended for use in basements. The ceiling cover is heavy, so consult an architect or an engineer if there is any possibility of structural problems. Soundproof the ceiling by filling the gap between the Sheetrock and the upper floor with insulation.

Miscellaneous: While acoustical tile and Sheetrock are commonly used for basement ceilings, there are other materials that will brighten up the darkest room of the house. Try painting the joists and the subfloor. In family rooms you can pick up accent colors and use one on the subfloor and another on the joists. There is little work involved and the effect is dramatic. Or, attach cork tile at right angles to the joists. You can cut the sound that filters upstairs, and provide a smashing contemporary look. Or attach boards or lath strips to the joists at right angles for a 'natural' textured look that will spark both conversation and decoration. However, always keep in mind that you should have some form of fireproofing—to protect the rest of the house. Don't let this stop you from having that imaginative-looking ceiling, but make certain that you consult an expert.

Details and appointments: Any basement conversion requires finishing touches to complete the project. Don't overlook adequate lighting. This means adequate wiring. Seek professional advice—a lighting contractor or electrical contractor—before you start your remodeling. Plan for a contemporary look. Install lighting between the floor joists with a luminous panel or use drop lighting. Look at all the alternatives available—surface fixtures, pendants, light tracks, and recessed units.

There are other ways to add light to your basement, too. By the outer wall below the ceiling, remove the blocking between joists and replace it with glass or Plexiglas. Create a small garden-under-ground with a window well. (See example in the next section.) Or, excavate and install steps down to the basement. This last suggestion affords you an outside entryway for the basement and allows you to bring materials in and out of your basement, besides providing basement lighting. Whatever method you use, always consult an expert.

Where to get help: Scratching your head when confronting a basement remodeling won't get the job done. There are sources that will provide you with all the necessary information.

Design help: You know what you want, so take all the ideas you get from flipping through magazines or books to your building contractor. He can translate your ideas into finished projects or advise you on how to get them done. Often, he has a design service available. For a complicated project, enlist the aid of an architect or a building designer.

Construction help: For many small jobs, you can do the work yourself. But for major projects, consider a remodeling contractor. Consult friends and neighbors for advice about builders who have done similar work.

Don't hesitate to ask the builder to show you examples of work that he has done—he'll be only too happy to help. Or ask your local building materials dealer. If you still need help, call the local chapter of the National Association of Home Builders. They'll give you a list of members who do remodeling.

Materials help: Your local lumberyard or building supply dealer should be able to furnish you with the materials you need. If not, write to the manufacturer of the material. For special materials, write to one of the material's associations, such as the American Plywood Association, Western Wood Products Association, National Floor Covering Institute, or National Paneling and Hardwood Manufacturers Association. All have materials booklets that will be of help to you.

Planning—some cautions: Before you start hammering and sawing, make a plan of your basement and try to visualize what you want to go where. All the while keep in mind several facts that may save you time and money:

Plumbing: Don't put your laundry center or half-bathroom in the opposite corner to the central water and waste supply. Otherwise, you'll have to invest in long runs of expensive water and waste piping.

Venting: If you want to install a fireplace in the new basement family/game room, make sure that you are able to vent a flue to the outside. The same holds true for a dryer vent.

Water Seepage: Don't be fooled into covering over the cracks in the floor or wall. You'll discover they've spread when your basement is flooded. Get rid of the cause of the seepage before you lay the carpet or install paneling.

Power: You can't run many power tools on 110 volt lines, so have a line installed, or set up your workshop close by a laundry where there is a line for adequate power.

Sound: Avoid placing a 'noisemaker'—a laundry, family room, workshop, or game room—beneath a formal room. It's difficult to filter out all sound—including the hum of a washer or dryer—but you can cut it to a minimum. Add further protection with acoustical tile.

Safety: Don't take risks with wiring and plumbing. The money you save today is probably the money you'll have to put out later to repair damage caused by a fire or a cracked pipe—or to satisfy a building or loan inspector. Have a professional do the work—he'll be aware of local codes and safety.

Don't put a workshop close to a heat unit. Sawdust will filter through the system and into other areas of the house. As sawdust is combustible, this poses a potential fire hazard.

Locate your laundry center close to the stairs. It's not fun lugging a heavy basket of wash from the far corner of the basement and up the stairs to closets and dressers.

Take note, too, of the following sizes. Include them in your plan.
• Ceiling height. Allow at least 81 inches.
• Clothes closets. Allow a maximum depth of 24 inches for suits and dresses.
• Door opening. Should be 30 inches minimum.
• Freezer. Normally is 27½ inches wide, 37½ inches deep, and 25 inches high.
For a larger unit, allow 71x32x37 inches. Uprights range from 24x29x57 to 32x21x66 inches. Get specs from dealer.
• Pool tables. Allow minimum of 54 inches from both sides and 66 inches if there are chairs located around the table.
• Sewing centers. Allow a total of 72x36x36 inches for layout purposes.
• Stair width. Should be 36 inches.
• Table tennis. Must have 10 feet from table ends to the wall, and 72 inches from sides to the wall for player movement.
• Washer/dryer. Usually 60 inches total space, but remember that some units open from the front, others from the top.
• Work benches. Allow for a top of 24 inches and a height of 32 inches.

Glossary

Anchor bolt (or screw)—bolt or screw to attach furring or other objects to a masonry surface such as poured concrete or block.

Battens—wooden or metal strips that are fastened over joints to hide the joints. Battens usually are installed vertically.

Blocking—a member between ends of floor joists that provides rigidity for joists. Sometimes called "crossbridging."

Flange-type screw—used mainly for plaster or gypsum wallboard for greater strength. Tightening spreads the arms of the flange so that it bears against the backside of the plaster holding the object very rigid.

Floor joist—horizontal member supporting a floor. In a basement, a ceiling joist.

Foundation wall—a masonry wall used as a support for space above and for the enclosure of basement space: it is made up of concrete block (7⅝x15⅝x8 inches), clay tile, placed concrete (no mortar joints).

Furring strip—wood, metal, or other material that is applied to a wall surface to even it or provide the surface for fastening of another material such as paneling or gypsumboard.

Insulation board—is usually used as a sheathing material. It is generally 25/32 inches thick in 4x8-foot sheets. It is a low density material made of wood, sugarcane, cornstalks.

Hardboard—generic name for a number of boardlike materials made up of fibers or wood chips. Can be finished or unfinished. There are standard and tempered types. Tempered hardboard is more moisture resistant and slightly higher in cost than the standard type. Both types may be purchased in plain, smooth sheets or perforated for use in workshops and special storage areas.

Hopper window—window hinged at the bottom, which opens into a room. In the basement, usually at the ceiling line.

Lath—a base for plaster walls. It may be strips of wood, metal gypsum, or insulation board for plaster. Today, lath is generally used as a decorative treatment—especially in wood and metal forms.

Mullion—wooden or metal material that is located between openings of a window frame.

Pier—usually a column of masonry such as placed concrete, concrete blocks, or bricks used to support structural members.

Pipe column (or lally column)—cylinderical steel column used to support a beam on which a joist or another structural member rests.

Shim—a thin strip of metal or stone used for leveling. Shingles are used for shims.

Sleeper—strip of wood laid on a bare floor to which sub or finished flooring is nailed.

Trougher—a recessed channel concealing wiring or plumbing or lighting fixtures.

Subflooring—dimension lumber or plywood, usually, over which a finish floor is laid.

Veneer—materials can be thin strips of wood or masonry materials. Material generally is applied as a finish for walls, counter fronts and countertops. Hardwood plywood has a top layer of hardwood veneer.

Ideas at a Glance

Here are problem-solvers for basement conversions: wall and ceiling treatments, lighting, storage. You can use most any building material in the basement, if moisture problems are solved. For problem areas, buy some moisture-resistant materials.

For more light, a window well was constructed here (above). Part of the foundation had to be removed professionally for a steel window insert. The walls of the well are lined with Roman brick. Enough light filters in the well for plantings. A drain was installed in the bottom of the well to funnel away excess rainfall and moisture.

Understair area makes an excellent spot for a home office or study area. Back of the steps was covered with a ¾-inch-thick piece of plywood to accommodate built-in shelving. The covering also helps to deter dust and noise from the steps. Desk is standard size, fitted into the opening. Wiring is concealed in back of the desk.

Hard-to-cover basement walls are easy with colorful canvas panels, laced to spring-loaded poles sandwiched between 1x3 strips across the joists and floor (above). This idea is especially good for walls with moisture problems, since the canvas doesn't have to touch the foundation.

Regular cedar siding was used as a wall treatment in this basement room. The ceiling is covered with 1x3 slats of cedar material. The materials then were sealed with a clear penetrating stain to deter moisture and to make cleaning easier. Three rows of floor joists were left open and painted an accent color; the lights are typical basement fixtures wired in a series of four on a single toggle switch.

Wet bar that fits snugly under the stairway brings colonial America into the basement. All lumber is rough-cut. Antique strap hinges decorate the bar and used bricks set off the floor. Tapped into plumbing, sink is hidden under the mirror. Light-weight simulated beams were used.

Top of basement stairs houses drawbridge closet counterbalanced by weights in the wall. The walkway is made of 2x4 framing, ½-inch plywood with nonskid pads, and a facing of ½-inch plywood. Pull down on iron strip along door top with pole hook opens up the storage unit.

Workbench of one sheet of 4x8-foot, ¾-inch plywood, 3x4-foot, ⅛-inch pegboard, 2x4s, 1x4s, 1x2s, four feet of ¾-inch dowel, bolts, nuts, screws. Tool board has 4-foot fluorescent fixture mounted on 1x4 arms at the top of the tool panel.

Here's how workbench and tool storage plan goes together. To deter moisture, paint the toolboard both sides. Bench is bolted together at joints for knock-down feature. Cover the bench top with ¼-inch tempered hardboard.

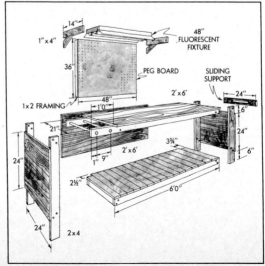

This kids' clubhouse looks expensive, but it isn't. Use 2x4s on edge of platform frame; ¾-inch plywood for deck. Attach frame to concrete walls with heavy screws and anchors; nail to wall studs. Band platform edging with 1x2s. Ladder is of 2x6s with 2x4 crosspieces. Sand wood; enamel.

Again, the playroom appears expensive and complicated—but it's neither of these. This time, a small section of the family room has been cornered off for a kids' study/mother's sewing center. Plentiful drawers, shelves, and cupboards keep everything neat yet handy. Because of the double-duty of this area, care was taken to make it both attractive and easy to keep clean.

Garage Remodeling

Other than providing shelter for the family automobile, most garage space is unorganized storage space that, with a little planning, could be turned into valuable work, living, or play space. The only basics you need are adequate lighting and heating—not a big expense when you tap into the house supply. Here's some planning help for your remodeling.

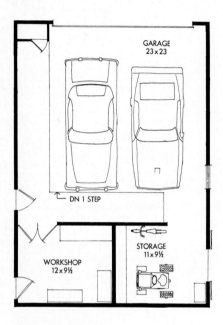

Two-car garages lend themselves to both workshop and lawn and garden storage, since they're usually plenty large. Here, a roomy shop and storage area was built into the rear of the garage by simply adding two partition walls and three doors. If your space is limited, consider the workshop plan shown at right. The partition wall is framed with 2x6 end uprights and 2x4 studs between. The top half of the wall is skinned with ¼-inch perforated hardboard; from the floor to the bench height, ¼-inch-thick exterior plywood was used. The workbench framing is tied into the 2x6 uprights, and framed out with 2x4s. The bench top is a solid core door topped with ¼-inch tempered hardboard, which can be removed easily when it becomes worn. Floor is tiled; ceiling is left open for overhead materials storage such as long 2x4s.

Shop Storage Area

Garage space makes excellent workshop space because noise and fine, airborne sawdust are confined 'outside' main living areas.

Since your space allotment is predetermined, you should take time to preplan on paper where workbenches, tables, power equipment, and storage should be located. To achieve a smooth-working shop, divide existing space into areas so you won't be stacking projects and building on top of yourself. Keep hand tools in one area and power tools in another. If space is tight, you might consider putting stationary-type power equipment on casters so it can be moved into position or out of the way, depending on your current projects.

For lots of light and ventilation (the more, the better), you may be able to cut in a large window for the shop area and add an extra-wide access door for moving big materials in and big projects out.

Typical builder's house has attached two-car garage with an overhead door. To remodel the garage into the family room plan below, the garage door was removed and replaced with double windows and matching vertical siding. An additional storage area was built onto the rear of the garage for outdoor furniture and lawn and garden equipment that was once stored in the garage area. Since garage adjoined 'wet wall' in the kitchen (most plans like this do), it was no problem to connect into the existing plumbing for a wet bar in one corner. For heating, gas-fired vents were installed; gas supply pipes were threaded over the ceiling and down the sidewalls. Standard building materials were utilized inside: gypsumboard walls and ceiling, a resilient tile floor, and prefabricated cabinets. A simple storage wall was built on one wall.

Expand for Family Room

If you're hunting for inexpensive living space that's already built, don't overlook your attached garage. Chances are it can be converted quickly into a family room by simply removing the garage door and filling in the space with matching siding and finishing off the interior with gypsumboard and flooring.

If your present furnace unit has the capacity to heat the space, extend ducts from the present system. If not, install a separate heating/cooling unit in the room. Electricity is easy to bring into the space; plumbing supply lines also can be extended.

The driveway may be used as an off-street parking facility. The secret to making it look like one is to break out about six feet of the driveway next to the house and plant the area with shrubs and flowers. The edge of the driveway can be finished off with a redwood strip on edge.

Fill-in siding, windows, doors, and outdoor lighting should match the same products used for the rest of your home. Don't mix them or attempt to change the basic architectural lines. To match the siding for the garage door fill-in, you can remove old siding from the rear of the house. This way, the wood matches as to style and weathering characteristics.

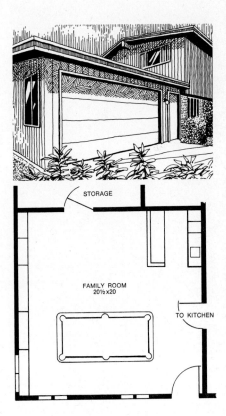

Special Rooms

Only 9x12 feet of garage space was sectioned off for the sewing room. There's plenty of footage left to park the family car and store bikes, outdoor furniture, and lawn and garden equipment. Roll-around table—a base cabinet on casters with an extended top provides additional counter area.

The dead space you often have in a garage can be put to good use: turn it into that long-needed sewing center.

To build this sewing center, a room was created inside the garage, taking advantage of unused space. More efficient lawn and garden storage was created, too, since junk, tools, and whatnot usually expand to fill any available space as any homeowner knows.

Standard 2x4 partition walls enclose the sewing center; 2x6 joists on 24-inch centers were added overhead to support the insulated gypsumboard ceiling. Although not quite as convenient as before the remodeling, the same entry door to the house was used with another door entry from the garage area.

Existing garage wiring was beefed up to handle the center's electrical needs, and heating/cooling ducts were extended through the wall from an adjoining kitchen. The built-ins are prefabricated cabinets; size of the room was worked out on a module system so that standard materials and cabinets could be used throughout, reducing costs and building time. Soffits hide fixtures for soft, indirect lighting.

Select the Right Materials

Finishing or remodeling your garage for more living space is easy. If you are reasonably handy with tools and have a basic knowledge of construction techniques, there's no reason why you can't close up a doorway, add a door or window, install gypsumboard, or tile a floor. Codes in your area may restrict you from running in wiring, plumbing, and heating; you can, however, add the finishing touches to these installations after the professionals make the initial hookups.

Closing in the garage: When your plans are firm and you have obtained any necessary building permits, the first step is to close in the garage. Once you've done this, you'll be able to work in almost any weather, at nights —whenever you want. Removing the garage door and installing new siding is a weekend job. You'll need a helper or two to handle the door since it is very heavy.

To remove the door, first open it, then release the springs that hold it in balance. This usually involves bolt-type releases on the ends of the springs. Close the door and remove the rollers on each side of it. These are bolted in place. You now can lift the door away from the tracks. The rollers will be in the tracks.

Remove the tracks, then the trim boards around the opening. Go easy with your pry bar; you may be able to use some of the boards later in construction. When the trim is off, you'll probably find a double 2x8 or 2x10 header and double 2x4 studs, which frame in the opening.

To close in the wall, you will need a sill plate to span the distance between the 2x4 jams. Get one that is the width of the sill already in place, usually a 2x6 or 2x8.

Anchor the sill to the concrete, using cedar shingle shims to level it. For fasteners, you may use lag bolts and lead expansion anchors. You'll have to drill holes for these in the concrete. Countersink the heads of the lag bolts, if they are in the way of stud placement. When you set the sill, use a thin piece of insulation under it. You can buy insulation made especially for this purpose.

Frame in the opening with 2x4 studs placed 16 inches on center. Toenail the studs to the header and the sill. Then apply sheathing to the outside of the framing. This may be plywood or insulation board. The finish siding goes over the sheathing. If the siding is plywood, it's easy to match it with the adjoining siding. If the siding is shingles or lap siding, you may have to juggle several courses to match it perfectly. Don't apply it in a straight vertical line because this line will always show.

Install windows and doors next. You can buy pre-hung doors and windows, which usually are framed in the openings with double 2x4 headers, jambs, and, for windows, sills. So all you have to do is, cut out the opening, flash it with asphalt building paper, and insert the door or window units. Fasten them to the jambs, header, and sill.

The framing of many garages consists of 2x4 studs on 24-inch centers. Since a roof structure is the only weight involved, this spacing is adequate. You should, however, fill in the framing with additional studs, spaced in 16-inch centers and toenailed to the headers and sills. Also give the ceiling rafters the same reinforcement, if they are in 24-inch centers. This is a 'fill-in' job; you can buy precut studs and rafters to span the gaps, eliminating a lot of extra sawing and fitting.

Floor treatments: Garage floors are usually one step below the entrance level to a home. You can either raise the floor to the same level or leave the step; this may depend on the amount of headroom you have in the garage. If you have the room and want to raise the floor, you can do this with 'sleeper' blocks, which form the framing for the subfloor. Here are the basic techniques for this installation:

Seal the surface of the concrete with sheets of polyfilm vapor barrier. Small daubs of tile mastic will hold the film in place. Don't rip the material; if you do, patch it. Patch any big concrete breaks.

To support the subfloor, lay 2x4s, 2x6s, or 2x8s on edge in rows across the floor. The dimension of the lumber you use depends on how high you want to raise the floor. The rows should be on 12-inch centers. Since the garage floor will be uneven in spots, you'll have to level the sleepers, using cedar shingle shims. Then 'tack' the sleepers to the floor with concrete nails or nails fired from a nail gun. Fastening the sleepers at the ends first provides enough rigidity to permit additional nailing across the room without slippage.

You can buy sleepers with synthetic rubber cushions on the underside of them; these will give the floor resilience. Toenail the sleepers to the sills, and, if possible, to the studs.

To prevent lateral movement, install blocks between the sleepers. The blocks should be random-spaced and nailed into position similar to fire blocking in stud walls or bridging across joists. Use plenty of blocks.

Depending on how your garage is framed and finished, you may be able to use joist hangers for the sleepers. Simply nail the hangers to the framing or ledges.

Install plumbing, heating, and wiring between the sleeper joists at this point in construction. When you have had it roughed in, install insulation between the sleepers. Use vermiculite fill, batt, blanket, or loose-fill fiberglass insulation. If the insulation has a reflective covering on it, make sure the reflective covering faces the warm side of the room.

For the subfloor, use ¾-inch-thick plywood sheathing. Do not install this material, however, until all wall framing has been completed.

Make all cutouts in the sheathing for heating ducts, plumbing, and electrical outlets, and nail the sheathing to the sleepers with threaded nails, countersinking the nails below the surface of the plywood. This will deter nail 'pops' in future years.

Install the finish floor over the sheathing. Make this the last job you do in the room.

Flooring products suitable for use in garages include resilient tile, hardwood blocks, hardwood strips, vinyl sheets, and carpeting. Since the floor is above-grade, there are no restrictions on the type of flooring you purchase.

Some products, however, require an underlayment such as asphalt building paper or padding. Your floor covering dealer will advise you as to the type of underlayment needed for the floor covering you choose.

Wall treatments: After you have reinforced the garage walls with additional framing have the wiring, heating, and plumbing installed. Then tack on the insulation. Most insulation (batts, rolls) is marked as to the side that should face the warm side of the room. You may even want to use Styrofoam insulation, which is usually installed with adhesive.

If the garage has been finished inside with gypsumboard, chances are the garage has been insulated. You can check this easily by drilling a small hole in the wall and taking a look. If you don't find insulation, you will have to have a professional do the work for you. Loose-fill insulation is the best solution here, as it can be blown between the studs with special equipment.

Wall coverings for garages range from gypsumboard to paneling to simulated brick and stone. Gypsumboard and paneling are the most common types of materials used; special accents usually are applied over the gypsumboard sheets. Check the instructions.

To install gypsumboard, nail it directly to the studs with special nails made for this material. Then cement and tape the joints; you should buy cement and tape made for gypsumboard. The dealer will outfit you.

Taping joints is fairly simple, although you'll have to practice a couple of times to get the tape smooth. First, fill the joint and edges of the gypsumboard with the cement, which is about the consistency of spackling compound. Then, embed the tape into the fresh compound, at the top of the joint, and, with a wide scraper, run the tape down the joint in a sweeping motion. The tape is perforated, so the cement, under the pressure of the blade, squeezes through the holes and forms a bond. Until you get the hang of it, the tape probably will wrinkle. If it does, keep pulling up and seating the tape until it is smooth. When the cement is dry—wait a day or so—sandpaper (medium on a block) the wall smooth.

If the interior surfaces will be gypsumboard, install the panels on the ceiling first —then the sidewalls. The nailing and joint treatment are the same. You can buy thin metal angles for inside and outside corners, which when nailed into position serve as sort of a trim piece to bind the panels. Apply cement and tape over the angles for a smooth job.

Wood paneling can be installed directly over the studs, although for a quality job you should have a gypsumboard base. If you use gypsumboard, with paneling over it, you needn't cement and tape the joints. Simply apply the paneling with adhesive locked in a caulking gun frame.

With a gypsumboard base, any wall covering —wallpaper, contact paper, paint, simulated brick and stone, plastic sheets, or glass—can be applied directly to it. You should, however, seal the metal, since it has a paper covering. A coat or two of flat paint is adequate.

Ceiling treatments: Your new room can have a 'flat' ceiling or a vaulted one, depending on the style roof the garage has and on whether trusses or conventional framing was used.

Regardless of framing, the ceiling must be insulated before it is finished. If your plans call for ceiling lighting, rough in the wiring before you install any covering or insulation.

Ceiling tile, plain or acoustical, may be applied over 1x3 furring strips nailed to the rafters, eliminating gypsumboard. Or you may want a suspended ceiling system, which also eliminates the need for a gypsumboard covering, saving the cost of this installation.

Frame in soffits for indirect lighting and storage at the same time you reinforce the ceiling rafters and before you apply ceiling/ wall materials. Framing usually is 2x4s.

Other ceiling treatments over a gypsumboard base include paint, wallpaper, contact paper, plastic sheets, and so on.

Details and appointments: It may be possible to extend heating/cooling ducts, plumbing, and wiring into your garage conversion from your home. To find out for sure, consult professionals on this phase of the remodeling because your heating/cooling plant may not have enough capacity for the space. Plumb-

ing and wiring are less of a problem; however, codes in your community may have restrictions, so check them.

If you buy windows and exterior doors for your project, get the thermal type. Interior doors (usually hollow-core) come in a variety of styles and finishes to match almost any decorating scheme you may want.

Storage cabinets, wet bars, and built-ins should be framed in during the first phases of construction. But, if the cabinets are prefabricated and prefinished, you should nearly complete the remodeling job before you install them. This protects them from damage.

Where to get help: Architects, builders, and remodelers can help you with basic planning and construction of the project.

Select your materials at building supply outlets, general merchandise stores, and specialty building shops such as millwork outlets.

Plan your job: Sketch the job on paper, and work out a floor plan, utilizing dimensions of the furnishings you plan to put into the room.

Glossary

Blind nailing—to nail on paneling, molding, and other finishing materials so the nails don't show—usually at an edge.

Building paper—is a general term used for asphalt-impregnated paper (55-pound) that can serve as insulation. The paper is normally used for siding and roofing underlayment before these materials go on.

Fire stops—are blocks nailed between studs to deter the spread of fire.

Joint compound—a spackle-like material that is mixed with water—or is already mixed —for use in taping gypsumboard joints.

Lap siding—is often called bevel siding. It is created by resawing boards diagonally to produce a wedge shape similar to a cedar shingle or shake.

Lintel—is a horizontal framing member that usually supports a load over an opening such as a garage door, regular door, or window. Often called a 'header'.

Toenail—to nail a piece of material to another piece of material at an angle. The nail may or may not be countersunk.

Ideas at a Glance

Little, inexpensive finishing touches can give your garage remodeling a different dimension. Even a coat of bright-colored paint can spark up an otherwise dull room. Here are several suggestions you may want to incorporate into your remodeling. There are a couple of ideas, too, for better storage space, if you don't re-model your garage completely.

An indoor charcoal grill is a smart addition to a garage family room (right), if you do lots of enter-taining—and even if you don't! Many manufac-turers have prefabricated grill units that set in a base cabinet. Ventilation fans also are included. Special alcove was designed into this family room for a kitchen and barbecue setup. Simulated face brick was glued to the grill base and to wall above it. The cabinet doors are plywood with random grooves cut into them; floor is sheet vinyl.

Plant alcove was designed to be an integral part of the room in this remodeling. The framing is post-and-beam, using 4x4-inch posts. Inch-square wooden strips inside and outside hold the glass in the big frames. Tongue-and-groove boards were used for filler strips.

Wet bar and game storage is big feature of this garage family room remodeling. Cabinets in bar niche are prefabricated; game closet was framed with 2x4s. Closet doors are faced with the same paneling used in the room. The flooring is sheet vinyl. Note area spotlighting.

By replacing shingle siding on two sides of this garage (above), it was opened up for outdoor living. In summer months, the canvas curtains are drawn back so the garage may be used as a living area. When winter comes, the canvas is laced together for a weather barrier; the car is then parked inside. A flagstone patio adjoins area.

With perforated hardboard and a hopper-style box, it's easy to create a sports center in one corner of your garage (right). The hardboard is nailed to the studs. The hopper was fabricated from ¾-inch-thick exterior-grade plywood, glued and screwed together in butt joints. A bulletin board was added above the hopper.

If your garage has a pitched roof, you may want to duplicate this beamed ceiling idea. The beams are 2x10s spaced two inches apart. Regular tie rafters were substituted with 2x10s to carry out theme. Plywood was used for an accent wall and to form a base for the counter.

Big 4x4-inch posts provide the framing for this garage storage idea (below), adding a design flair as well as support for the shelves. The posts are butt-jointed with nails and toenailed into the wall framing and floor. Shelves were built from 4x8 sheets of exterior plywood sawed horizontally.

Attic Remodeling

An attic—like a basement—is bonus space. At first glance, you may think that your attic is too dark and small to convert it into livable bedrooms, a studio, home office, study, or playroom. This isn't necessarily so! A roof can be opened up with a dormer, or raised, for more space and light; ventilation, heating, and cooling can be added, too.

Additional Bedroom Space

Odd-shaped ceilings and walls can add architectural interest to your attic remodeling when roof lines can't be changed for a full-sized room. And if you are going to use the space for additional bedrooms, high ceilings really aren't necessary—especially for small children, who don't need the ceiling height. And, most kids' furniture usually is under-scaled, so space that may seem cramped to you becomes ideal for them.

To gain natural light, install prehung windows into the gable ends of the attic. The rest of the remodeling then becomes a simple cover-up job: finishing the walls, ceiling, and floor.

For heating and cooling, extend ducts between studs from a room below. And fish wires for lights up through a downstairs wall.

The long, narrow attic above was partitioned into two rooms: a bedroom and a play area. Odd angles created by roof pitch were turned into a lighting and decorating advantage. Bright, light-reflecting colors make the space seem larger than it actually is.

An operable skylight, hinged at the top, was installed in the roof for light and ventilation.

This knee wall (right) was covered with chalkboard material. Doodles can be erased with a damp sponge.

Although ceiling height wasn't standard in this attic conversion, there's plenty of headroom for youngsters. A partition wall created a niche for the dresser and a headboard for the bed. The ceiling and walls are covered with gypsumboard nailed to rafters and studs.

Studio Living Space

Many attics have plenty of headroom down the center of them, but not at the sides because of the roof pitch. If your attic has at least seven feet of headroom at the ridge, you can remodel it into a studio/living arrangement similar to the one here. If short on headroom, consider raising the roof a foot or so.

Furniture arrangement has been kept to the center of the attic, while knee walls have been utilized for storage, low cabinets, and television.

Here, two partition walls were built at the head of the stairsteps. The room across the 'hall' is a small sitting room. It is furnished with couches that make up into beds for overnight guests.

Both rooms were finished with gypsumboard, and each has plywood wainscoting topped off with a wide piece of molding. The knee walls are ideal for shutter-covered cabinets and drawers. The rooms were heavily carpeted and padded to muffle noise for the living areas below. Gable ends were opened up with windows.

Collar beams (the horizontal boards nailed to the rafters) may be raised a foot or so to provide more headroom. Construct knee walls out into the room so that there is at least four feet between the floor and where the ceiling starts. Partition the head of the stairwell to create a small hallway, even if the attic space will not be partitioned into separate living rooms.

Framing members of a dormer include (1) studs and rafters on 16-inch centers; (2) double headers above window openings; (3) double sills below window openings; (4) a double roof plate where the wall will be located; and (5) rafters that are supported by metal joist hangers.

Because of roof pitch and necessary building skills and equipment, dormer framing may be a job for a professional. You can add the finishing touches.

Refurbishing for Storage

Depending on the roof line, the space above your garage may be ideal for additional storage, and, perhaps, even an extra bedroom or living space. If you have some space now, you may be able to add more with a dormer similar to the one shown on this page.

Space too low here was converted into storage and the rest of the room into a playroom for the children. It also may be used as sleeping quarters for guests.

For a sitting area, a small dormer was added. It complements the architecture of the house and matches the other dormer in design.

For entry into the room, a doorway was cut into the wall separating the main house and the garage. The door is at the end of a hallway. Heating ducts were extended from the main house, and the wiring was hooked onto the circuit that runs into the garage space below. With plenty of insulation, the same heating and air conditioning system could be used. A bathroom was installed in one corner of the remodeling; supply lines run up through the garage.

Select the Right Materials

Two factors determine whether or not you can convert your attic into more living and/or storage space: accessibility and headroom. If you can't reach the attic from an interior stairwell, you'll have to build a stairway outside. And, if the ridge of the roof to the floor—from a point four feet out from each sidewall—doesn't measure at least seven feet, you will have to build on a dormer for the necessary headroom. These factors may limit your attic space to storage only.

Floor treatments: Any attic remodeling must start with the floor. Your present attic may already have a plywood or board subfloor. Or it may have several sheets of plywood or boards laid over the ceiling joists.

Before you lay down a permanent subfloor, install heating/cooling ducts, wiring, and plumbing between the joists. This might have been done when your home was built; if you can't tell for sure, check the plans or ask the builder, if you can find either of them.

When the 'mechanicals' are in, you should insulate the space between the joists. Use either loose-fill insulation for this (vermiculite or fiber glass) or batts and blankets, with the reflective side facing the attic room.

Lay the subfloor over the top edges of the rafters, and nail it in place with threaded nails, countersunk slightly below the surface of the wood. Sheets of ¾-inch-thick plywood are suitable for the subfloor, but you may want 1x4-inch tongue-and-groove lumber nailed across the joists.

At this point, do not cover the floor with any finish materials. The subfloor serves as a 'base' from which to work on the rest of the room. Install finish flooring after all the other work has been completed.

Building a dormer: If your plans call for a dormer, construct it first after you lay the subfloor, which serves as a working 'platform'.

This is not a complicated job. What sometimes makes it difficult for a handyman is the slope of the roof and the climate. If the pitch of your roof is not too steep, you may be able to rig the necessary scaffolding to frame and close in the dormer. Otherwise, turn the project over to a professional. Climate plays an important role, too. If you don't have the time to cut a hole in the roof, frame the dormer, and side it over in a period of several days, as rain may play havoc with the attic space and the structure of your home.

You'll need a dormer plan before you start work (if you plan to do it yourself). Match the dormer to the architecture of your home: the same type windows, siding, and roofing. The size of it depends, naturally, on the amount of space you want inside. When plans are complete, obtain a building permit, set up the scaffolding, and order all necessary materials. Because of the weather, there can't be any delays during initial construction.

Lay out the position of the dormer, and do all the framing you can inside the attic before you cut a hole in the roof. If you're going to build a shed-type dormer, it's best to double the side framing on the roof and notch the rafters to accept the dormer rafters. Also, prefabricate the front wall of the dormer and part of the roof, if possible.

When you have everything ready, strip off the roofing where the dormer will go, marking the corners on the roof with nails. With a chalk line, connect the corners; this will provide a sawing guide. With a portable electric saw or handsaw, cut away the sheathing. You'll need a helper in the attic to make sure you are following the exact measurements.

Brace the rafters around the opening you have just cut, *before* you remove the rafters in the space in which the dormer will be constructed. Use 2x4s for this, wedging them against the subfloor. From this point on, you will have to work fast to build the dormer and seal it against the weather. It's a good idea to have a waterproof tarp to cover the opening in the event of rain.

Double the rafters around the opening, extending them at least four feet beyond the top and bottom of the opening. This will provide extra strength. Also double the header and the sill at the opening for strength, if you didn't before you cut the opening in the roof.

Generally, it's best to build the front framing of the dormer first. Nail it in the correct position. Then, brace it with scrap 1x2s or other stock until the rafters are connected.

Install the new dormer rafters next. They run from the front framing back to a ledger strip that runs across the original roof rafters. Notch these rafters with a saw to fit the double framing or ledger strip. Nail them into position at the ledger strip, then fasten them to the front framing. You may be able to use metal joist hangers for the rafters at the ledger strip. You can notch the front of the rafters to fit the header of the front framing, if desired. Or you may toenail the rafters to the header. Either way, be sure to leave enough overhang or eave.

Frame in the sidewalls next. Construct the walls similar to partition walls—toenail them to the double framing at the opening in the roof and to the end rafters.

Sheathing goes over the framing; choose plywood, insulation board, or regular sheathing boards. Do the roof of the dormer first, then the sidewalls. Cover the sheathing with asphalt building paper. At the roof, where the dormer roof meets the house roof, waterproof the joints with a flashing material such as copper. In front, extend the flashing up under the siding, but over the shingles. At the sides, extend it under the siding and the shingles. Give the flashing a double coat of asphalt roofing compound to make sure it is waterproof. Use plenty of compound.

Install the roofing and siding to the dormer at this point. You'll probably have to juggle the courses of roof shingles back and forth so you get a good match and a waterproof job. Set them in the correct position before you attempt to final nail them in place. Daub the nailheads with asphalt roofing cement. If the front of the dormer will have siding, install the window unit before you nail on the siding, and flash the opening for the window with asphalt building paper. Then, insert the unit in the opening and fasten it.

Finally, install the soffit in the overhang, or box in the eaves. While you're on the roof, give the siding and the window a prime and finish coat of paint, if the materials are not prefinished or just preprimed.

Wall treatments: To achieve more light and better ventilation in the attic, you may want to put a window in the gable ends. If so, do this before doing any other remodeling work.

First, double the studs around the window opening, and use double 2x4s for the header and sill plates. You can frame this in before you cut the opening for the window.

To cut the opening, drill small holes at all four corners from the inside through the sheathing and the siding. This will establish the dimensions outside for the opening. Outside, remove the siding back to the vertical joints past the holes. This will expose the sheathing. Then, from the inside, saw out the opening for the window. Flash the opening with asphalt building paper and install the window, fastening it in position according to manufacturer's instructions. After fitting the new siding, caulk the joints around the window outside and add any necessary trim.

Wall coverings for your attic remodeling are almost limitless. Gypsumboard and paneling are quite popular because both are easy to install. If you use simulated brick or stone, glass, or plastic for accents, back these materials with a gypsumboard base for rigidity.

Additional framing may be necessary before any coverings are applied to the studs and rafters and any other basic framing.

Knee walls consist of 2x4s nailed to the rafters and to a 2x4 plate fastened to the plywood or board subfloor. Position the knee walls at least four feet out from the rafters into the room. The space behind the knee walls is ideal for storage. If you decide to use the space in this way, double the studs for cabinet doors, and leave additional room for extra-large drawers.

Collar beams or the roof rafters that run horizontally across the attic can be moved up slightly to achieve more headroom. However, you'll have to add more rafters on 16-inch centers because most unfinished attics use collar beams spaced on 24- or even 36-inch centers just close enough together for lateral support. If possible, try to make the distance between the sloping rafters—across the collar beams—in two- or four-foot modules. This way, you can save material and minimize cutting and fitting. You'll probably have to bevel the edges of the gypsumboard slightly to match the angle of the rafters. Or, if you can get a tight fit, just cement and tape the joint. Build partition walls before nailing on the wall covering of your choice. Frame these walls with 2x4 sills and headers, with studs on 16-inch centers. To compensate for the slope of the rafters, you may have to bevel the ends of the studs to fit the header.

Insulation goes between the rafters and studs after all the framing has been completed. Use blanket, batt, or rigid-type insulation, plenty of it. Only the roof and wallboard are between you and the weather outside. Your building material retailer will be able to specify the thickness of insulation (depends on climate) you need in the attic.

Ceiling treatments: Gypsumboard or ceiling tile is the best material for an attic ceiling. Both are quick to install—especially around skylights and over odd shapes and angles. Or, depending on the pitch of the roof, you may want to leave the rafters exposed for design purposes. If so, seal the rafters with a clear penetrating stain, or paint as an accent.

Exposed rafters may pose a heat loss problem, since regular insulation can't be used. However, you may be able to substitute rigid Styrofoam insulation sheets, fitted between the rafters and painted.

Skylights can help to provide additional natural light to an attic remodeling. In addition, they're easy to install on any type roof. You can buy them in two types: shed dormer and dome. The shapes are square, rectangular, and round; some models even provide ventilation.

To install a skylight, cut and tie off a couple of rafters, and box the opening with double framing. Skylights are usually designed to go across about three rafters, or 46 inches.

Drive nails through the roofing and sheathing at the four corners of the 'box'. The nails must go straight through; you should drill pilot holes for them so they go straight through.

On the roof, snap a chalk line between the protruding nail points. Take the skylight frame and fit it over the lines to make sure it fits correctly. Make any corrections at this point.

With a sharp razor or linoleum knife, cut the roofing away along the lines. You must leave any shingles that will overlap the flange of the skylight. If the roof is covered with wooden shingles, just pry off the ones involved and save them for later to fill in around the opening. Then, flash the opening, preferably with aluminum, if the skylight is aluminum.

With a saber saw or keyhole saw, cut through the sheathing, following the guide lines based on the nail points and frame.

The skylight fits into a metal frame, which is inserted into the hole and fastened to the sheathing and rafters. Metal flashing strips go under the roofing paper and up along the edges of the nailing strip. This should make the joints watertight.

When the frame is in and the dome is installed, carefully seal the flange, shingles, and flashing around the skylight with asphalt roofing compound or the type of mastic recommended by the manufacturer. Also seal all nailheads. If the unit has a ceiling fixture, it, too, fits into the frame. Caulk around the metal and wooden framing for weatherproofing and to keep out any attic dirt and dust.

Details and appointments: Stairsteps leading to your attic may already be installed, requiring only finishing. But, if the access is via a pulldown arrangement in a hallway, you will have to build a stairwell. Since the stairwell can't be in the middle of a hallway, you will have to spot it in a closet or borrow space from a room to build it.

You can buy prefabricated stairsteps or precut parts for stairsteps. You'll need to tell the dealer the distance from the floor to the ceiling where the steps will go into the attic and the width of the stairwell.

The steps are supported by two carriages, which are nailed to opposite walls. You'll probably have to build a standard partition wall to support one carriage.

At the ceiling, cut an opening into the ceiling covering, and tie off the joists with double headers. Use double joists at the side of the opening, too, for more support.

Fasten the treads and risers to the carriage pieces with finishing nails. If your project calls for a landing, build this with 2x8s, skinned with ¾-inch plywood. Then, toenail it to the flooring, counter sinking the nail heads.

Heating may be extended up through ducts in rooms below. Simply run a duct between the studs into the attic space. Or, you may want to heat and cool the area with a separate unit. You have a heating advantage in the attic, as heat rises from the downstairs rooms. Cold, however, drops from air conditioning units. Keep basement doors closed.

Lighting and convenience outlets in the attic are no trouble to install, since you usually can run a separate circuit from the main electric entry up through the walls into the attic. Then, junction off the power for specific purposes. Use flexible conduit for this.

Standard fixtures work well in the attic. However, you may have to settle for recessed or flat fixtures because of headroom space problems, so measure before you buy.

Plumbing, like wiring, may be extended into the attic fairly easily, especially if you run it up from a 'wet wall' below. Plan an attic bathroom so it is directly above the bathroom below—or near it.

Where to get help: If your attic remodeling will require a dormer, contact a builder, or architect for planning and design help. Since you are going to change the structure of your home, this type of addition has to be engineered. Even if you do all of the work yourself, it's best to have blueprints to follow. You'll save many costly errors.

Your building supply dealer also will be able to help you with design; he probably even knows a reputable architect, builder, or remodeler, if you plan to have part of the job done professionally.

Interior decorators and magazines and books devoted to remodeling subjects are other good design idea sources. Don't overlook scouting trips through model homes, either. Many have attics that have been finished; these may supply you with some ideas, too.

Plan your job: Although you may not have any major structural changes, you should pre-plan your attic remodeling project on graph paper before you order any materials or cut a board. Attic space is especially critical as to measurements, since ceiling heights and angles can restrict the use of some materials and furnishings you have planned on.

Any structural changes or the addition of plumbing, wiring, or heating/cooling may require a building permit. Obtain the permit from the city; you usually have to submit some sort of plan or blueprint to be issued a permit. A builder or architect will know the procedures.

Glossary

Baluster—is a small column or spindle that is used to support a stair railing or balcony. Balusters are sandwiched between a top and bottom rail and fastened.

Bevel board—used in framing in a roof or stairway. It serves as a template to lay out bevels and angles of construction.

Brace—is used to complete and support a triangle; framing lumber is fitted and fastened at any angle to strengthen the angle.

Carriages—stringers or supports for treads and risers of stairsteps.

Checkrails—are meeting·rails that fill the opening between top and bottom window sash created by the parting stop in the window frame. The rails usually are beveled.

Drip—is a sill or water table that permits water to drain away from the side of the house below. A groove is cut in the underside of the sill so the water will drop off the outer edge and clear the siding below.

Flashing—is strips of roofing or metal basically utilized to waterproof around chimneys, dormers, gutters, doors, and windows.

Jack rafters—are short rafters used between a wall plate and a hip rafter. They also are short rafters that form a gable or the start of a new roof line for an addition.

Landing—is a platform between different levels or flights of stairsteps. The platform also may be at the top and bottom of the stairs.

Ideas at a Glance

Details and appointments can make attic rooms more livable. Best yet, many items are not costly. For example, you can add brightness to a wall with paint. False beams made from Styrofoam look like the real thing, and they can turn an attic room into a handsome study area. The addition of a skylight or two can provide light and ventilation.

Attics are ideal for storage, too, since knee walls have to be constructed along the roof pitch. Use all sorts of drawer and door styles.

In this section you will find a potpourri of ideas that you can borrow or adapt to your special attic remodeling plans.

Here, a high ceiling was painted out with a neutral gray to make it less obtrusive. A red color accent was used to bring the eye down to the lower part of the room. The stairway in this attic is in the middle of the room. Two beds are in one section; a conversation area is located in the other. Division of the rooms is formed by the location of the stairs.

A rustic look was achieved in this attic remodeling for a boy's bedroom by leaving the rafters exposed. The rafters were stained the same color as the prefinished paneling, shelving, and wainscoting at the knee walls. The sheathing between the rafters was painted an accent color to help brighten the room. Area lighting was provided for a desk; the floor is carpeted to help deter sound.

Skylight arrangement runs along the ridge of the roof between rafters. The glass is double-insulated and installed in grooves cut into the rafters. For more support, small, square blocks of wood were nailed to the rafters next to the glass, and the panes were glazed outside to block moisture. Three prefabricated and laminated beams were used to frame in this custom-built skylight.

Massive skylight (right) is formed by removing every other rafter for the width required. The top and bottom of the opening, as well as the sides, are boxed with double wood framing. By cutting into the roof this way, you can convert minimum space into more living space without spending a lot of money. The area may be used for extra room for sleeping, as a hobby studio, or as a hideway for reading, music, or just relaxation. Insulated glass should be used for the lights. Here, a 2x4 was toe-nailed to the existing 2x6 joists or rafters to form a curb. The glass was laid over each member and then locked into position with 1x2-inch wooden stop. The glass was set in mastic, and mastic was used around the stop for weatherproofing purposes.

If you plan niches and offsets in four-foot modules, you can then utilize the space with prefabricated built-ins and furnishings. Most building is on a modular system in increments of two feet or four feet. Stick to this system, and other products will fit, such as this desk in a knee wall attic. Although the ceiling slants, there's still plenty of headroom without ducking.

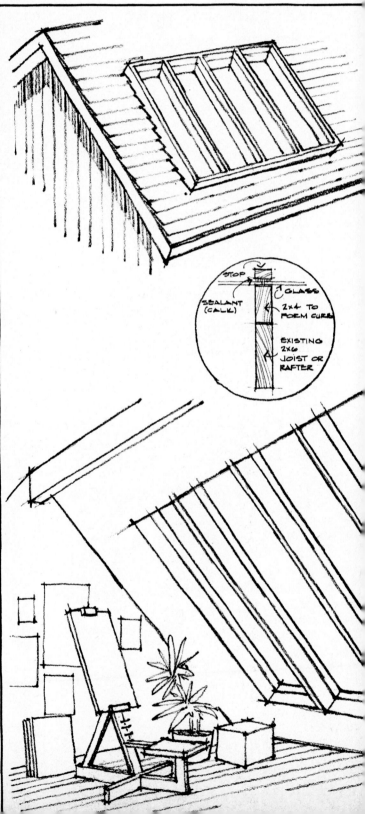

Here's a light and ventilation scoop arrangement utilizing dormer construction (right). The over-sized window is modern in design, complementing the furnishings in the room. Standard shed-roof construction was used for this application, with special flashing attention at sidewalls and the windows to block rain and melting snow.

Here's how a dormer can provide extra headroom and space to an attic room (above). For even more space, you may want to build a dormer on the opposite side of the room, extending the width of the room. Standard windows were used here to carry out the architecture of the house. Note the small storage area in the background. The door had to be cut at an angle to fit the slope. The floor is hardwood strips with area rugs.

Your slanted attic ceiling may need the bold approach. You can make it as compelling as a modern painting by covering the gypsumboard with a geometric-patterned wallpaper. If the room is small, big patterns give it added depth and disguise the odd-angle lines formed by the roof pitch. The black carpeting runs up the side of the bed, hiding the built-in frame. The thickness of the carpeting deadens sound below.

Laundry Room Additions

Because manufacturers have designed washers and dryers to fit small spaces, these appliances have been related to small space. And, as a result, the laundry center usually is located in a dark corner of the basement or utility room, and more often than not, it lacks adequate work space, lighting, and storage. Here's how you can make your laundry center more efficient.

In Basement

Basement space can be unorganized space, and most unorganized of all is the washer/dryer combination that is shoved over in a corner or behind the furnace. On washday, clothing is carried down, laundered, and carried upstairs to a kitchen or dining room table to be folded and crammed into a plastic basket for distribution to a linen closet or dresser drawer.

Building an efficient laundry center is, perhaps, one of the most inexpensive remodeling projects to do. It requires a minimum of planning, technical know-how, and standard materials that can be fabricated with basic hand tools and fasteners.

A case in point is this basement laundry room addition. The ceiling is gypsumboard painted white; the floor is vinyl strips; the walls are covered with vinyl wall covering; and the storage wall forms a divider.

Floor plan shows relationship of the laundry area and family room. Floor of the entire basement area was covered with the same sheet vinyl material, and the storage area was built over it. A solid-core door was covered with plastic laminate for a folding table; the storage shelves were built with sheets of ¾-inch exterior-grade plywood. Plywood also was used for the cabinet doors; hardboard for sliding ones.

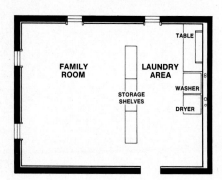

Clothes Care Center

Often, the simple things are the best, and this laundry center is simple: an in-line unit that features a matching washer/dryer; a cabinet for detergents and laundry accessories; and a closet for clothing, takedown ironing board, and portable sewing machine.

Indirect lighting was used between floor joists under a suspended ceiling. A prefabricated cabinet system was designed, utilizing ¾-inch exterior-grade plywood. The cabinet is simply a three-sided box with sliding and hinged doors attached to 2x4 framing members. Random-grooved ¼-inch paneling adds richness to the project; it is attached to furring strips.

The floor is sheet vinyl in a slate pattern; the cabinet unit has a 4-inch toe space to match that of the dryer. Aluminum channels were used as door slides for hardboard doors in the upper cabinets.

Top cabinets are designed not only for storage, but for indirect lighting for the appliances and accessory center.

The cabinet is not attached to the suspended ceiling; it is screwed to the partition walls for stability. A wide board was used between the cabinets and center below to provide unitized visual effect, tying in the entire cabinet area. Green color of the cabinet unit accents the dark color of the paneling, which is carried out on both sidewalls. Paneling also hides venting and electric wiring for appliances.

Using simple butt joints, glued and screwed together, was the only framing technique needed to assemble this in-closet storage area. The unit was prefabricated according to closet measurements, then slipped into position. Screws hold it tightly to the sidewalls; the doors are hinged to the edge of the 1x12 uprights. To deter moisture and make cleaning easier, the framing was given two coats of paint; the doors are painted to match.

In Closet

The proximity of a laundry center to where dirty linens and clothing are stored prior to washday may be an important consideration in your family. If so, opening up a double closet for appliances and accessories, as shown here, may be just the ticket for you.

Stackable appliances were used. The dryer is vented into an attic; the washer is hooked into an adjoining bathroom waste pipe. A simple framework of 1x12 pine boards was used to frame in the area for shelving and over-appliance storage. Louvered doors may be closed while the machines are operating; there's plenty of ventilation through the louvers. A nearby bathtub is utilized as a soaking facility.

Select the Right Materials

A laundry center should be just as handy for the homemaker as a workshop is for the home handyman. And because it is a center where the homemaker spends so much time, it should be attractive, too.

Before you start buying materials, take stock of the area you'll use. Design out dampness and improper venting and wiring, and plan for adequate lighting and storage—include also tabletop space.

Especially, get rid of any dirt-makers. Dirt and dust are the biggest enemies of a washer and dryer. They clog up machines and foul up water drainage. And while you're doing that, make sure the dryer is properly vented and grounded to prevent electrical shock.

Floor treatments: Even with proper venting and drainage, a laundry center adds moisture to the area in which it is located. It is important to keep this moisture at a minimum by stopping any seepage through basement or on-grade floors. If the floor is brick, block, or dirt, replace it with concrete.

Concrete floors sometimes let in water through cracks and breaks in the floor and at the joints where the floor butts against the wall. A 'sweating' floor may be dried out through proper ventilation or a dehumidifier. Running water through joints may be caused by hydrostatic pressure outside the foundation wall, inadequate roof drainage, or flow-back of water from a badly sloped grade level.

You may be able to control hydrostatic pressure by cleaning out the damaged joint with a cold chisel and pressing hydraulic cement into the joint. Also check the gutters and downspouts outside to make sure they're not leaking water into the foundation wall, and slope the ground away from the foundation. But keep the ground six inches from the bottom course of wooden siding so moisture doesn't damage the siding.

Preparation of the floor is the key to installing most any floor covering, whether it's in the basement, living room, or garage.

For concrete floors, fill all cracks and holes with latex-based cement. Undercut the cracks in an inverted V with a cold chisel. This provides the best bond.

Remove all wax, grease, oil, and flaking paint. If you are going to install resilient tile over a painted concrete surface, you will have to remove the paint with a power sander. Use No. 5 or No. 4 abrasive (open coat) paper for this. You may not have to remove rubber-base paint. Check the flooring manufacturer's recommendations for preparation.

The flooring products you can use in a laundry center—or most any room anywhere—include inlaid vinyl flooring; rotogravure vinyl; linoleum, vinyl tile; matched tile in vinyl that looks like solid sheet when laid; asphalt tile; wax-free sheet flooring; and seamless flooring.

Floors of hardwood, slate, carpeting, and hardwood blocks also can be used in a laundry center, but they are not recommended because of the moisture problem, and cleaning and maintenance that is required.

As a rule, you can't install tile over existing tile, if the underfloor is in contact with the ground. This would include a basement installation. However, if the floor is suspended, you may install resilient tile over existing resilient floors of rubber, cork, solid vinyl, asphalt, linoleum, and vinyl asbestos tile. Caution: lay asphalt tile over existing asphalt or vinyl asbestos tile only; do not put it over existing cork tile since it might pop off.

If plans call for laying new tile over old in the laundry addition, do not lay the joints of the new tile directly over the joints of the old, existing floor.

Procedures for laying tile are simple. Almost the same rules apply for sheet goods.

First, prepare the subfloor, making sure it is squeaky clean. Then, lay out the room area. Find the center point of the room by measuring to the center point of each wall. Snap a chalk line between these points. The point at which the lines cross is the center point of the room or area you will cover.

With a carpenter's square, check the lines at the center point, making sure the lines are perfectly straight. This is important, since a crooked line can throw the measurements off for the rest of the room.

Check the lines again by laying down a row of tiles (no mastic) along the chalk line to the center point on opposite walls.

If the measurement between the wall and the last tile you put in position is less than three inches or more than nine inches, move the center line six inches closer to the opposite wall. Then snap a new chalk line. This procedure will improve the look of the floor. It also will keep you from having to cut and fit small pieces of tile next to the wall surfaces.

Start laying the tile, after you are certain your measurements are correct, by spreading mastic in one quarter of the area. Don't do the whole thing at once. Use a notched adhesive spreader and the type of mastic that is recommended by the flooring manufacturer.

Lay the first tile at the center line. Make sure this tile is set perfectly; it is the base point for all other tiles. If it is out of line, all other tiles will be out of line.

Set the rest of the tiles in the area. Lay the tile gently against the preceding tile, making sure the joint is a tight fit. Don't slide the tile in position; this may loosen the mastic and cause it to squeeze up through the joint.

Finish the area, one quarter at a time, and when this is completed, roll the floor with a rolling pin or roller you can rent for this purpose. Do not roll asphalt tile. It is brittle and may break under the pressure. If you use peel-and-stick tile, follow the same procedures outlined above. But go slow. Once the tile is down, you seldom can move it.

Remove any excess adhesive from the face of the tile when the floor is down and rolled. You may buy cleaners for this. Some adhesives can be removed with soap and water.

Strip flooring is similar to resilient tiles, except it is in rolls instead of squares. Floor preparation is the same as for tile. You may need an underlayment of felt for strip flooring. Your flooring dealer will know the answer to this problem and help you with it.

Warm strip flooring is easier to work with than cold material; let it set in a 70-degree room for 24 hours before you start working. Then unroll the flooring and cut it to the length of the room. Since strip flooring is costly, be sure your measurements are correct before you make any cuts. Fit one end of the material tightly against the wall of the room before you cut the other end.

Adhesive made for strip material is applied to the floor with a notched spreader. Do one strip at a time, spreading the adhesive evenly over the floor surface.

Press the flooring in position, along a perfectly straight chalk line you snap before the adhesive is applied. The edge of the flooring should follow the line; if not, pull up the strip and press it into position again. Like tile, the first strip of flooring has to be square or the other strips will be out of alignment.

Felt is laid with a special adhesive. Apply it evenly over the floor in a thin coating. Do not overlap the felt. Butt the joints like wallpaper. Also, put it down one-half length at a time. This will deter wrinkling.

For obstructions such as pipes, you can make a paper template and transfer the design of the obstruction on the flooring. Then make the necessary cuts. You may use the template technique for any flooring.

Seamless flooring may be purchased in a kit. Before installing this flooring, you have to have a clean surface, properly patched. Then mix the multicolored flakes together. Use a big plastic bag for this.

Cover any surface you don't want the seamless flooring to stick to—walls next to the floor, for example, and moldings.

Then apply the first coat of plastic to the floor. Spread it evenly over the surface. Let the first coat dry. Then, apply the second coat of laminating plastic to the base coat. Work in small areas with the second material.

Spread the flakes over the wet coat of plastic. Make sure the floor surface is thoroughly covered with the multicolored flakes.

When the floor is dry, lightly sand the floor to remove any loose flakes and those projecting above the plastic surface. Use a medium-grade, open-coat abrasive for the sanding operation. Do not oversand the area; once-over-lightly is plenty. Clean away all debris with a vacuum cleaner. Top coat the surface with two or more coats of the plastic laminate.

Wall treatments: Because of moisture, the preparation of basement walls for a laundry center is critical, unless you place the laundry in a closet, on a landing, in the corner of a garage, in the kitchen, or in the bathroom.

Patch any cracks in a masonry-type wall such as concrete block, placed concrete, brick, glazed tile, or gypsumboard.

If there is a water problem, you will have to correct it before applying any finish wall covering to the wall.

Most patches can be made by undercutting the cracks with a cold chisel and filling the cracks with latex-based concrete or spackling compound—if the wall is gypsumboard or plaster. If concrete, use a cement mixture.

Sometimes, builders leave concrete block or concrete walls with little daubs of concrete sticking to them. You can remove these humps and bumps with an abrasive brick you can buy for this purpose. Or use a No. 5 abrasive (open-coat) stretched over a piece of 2x4-inch scrap lumber for a sanding block.

Moistureproof the wall with a coat or two of moisture-resistant paint. This is recommended even if you don't have a moisture problem, as the paint provides a good work base, besides preventive action.

Wall covering materials are as plentiful as their floor counterparts. The problem here is mostly one of choice rather than installation techniques, which are simple.

For basement laundry areas, you may choose paneling, hardboard paneling, ceramic tile, plastic laminate, siding, gypsumboard, or just plain paint to add sparkle.

Panel materials and tile should be either furred out from the wall or attached to gypsumboard. Since pipes and hoses and electrical wiring may be in the way, you may have to use 2x4s fastened to the wall in vertical positions on 4-foot centers. Then notch the 2x4s with a saw and chisel to fit around pipes and other obstructions.

Coat the furring strips with a moisture-resistant paint before you fasten them to any basement wall. Or use a clear sealer.

If the wall is concrete blocks, you may use toggle bolts to fasten on the furring strips. Or, you can use lead anchors tapped into small holes drilled in the concrete. Use screws to fasten on the furring, turning the tips into the anchors. The same technique may be used for solid concrete walls, glazed tile, or brick. Toggle bolts or molly anchors may be used if the wall is gypsumboard. Make sure all furring strips are level and/or plumb (vertically level).

Finish materials, regardless of where they will be applied, should be moisture-resistant for a laundry center. Most paneling is prefinished. Give the back of it a coat of penetrating sealer. You can buy gypsumboard with a special moisture-resistant paper covering for this use. It comes in several thicknesses.

Storage walls may be fabricated from ¾-inch-thick plywood or a framework of 2x4s covered with hardboard, plywood, or gypsumboard panels. Or you can use dimension lumber.

Plywood is probably the easiest material for a handyman with basic tools to use. It is thick and rigid enough to be joined with simple butt joints, screwed and glued together. Cover exposed edges with a thin tape you can buy for this purpose, or fill with wood putty, then sand and paint. Or, you can cover the edges with moldings nailed into position and stained or painted to match the storage center.

Plywood also may be used for shelving. Or you can buy dimension lumber for shelving. Prefabbed shelving is available, too.

If you are going to frame in a cabinet, use 2x4s for the base and smaller members (1x3s or 1x4s) for crosspieces and trim. The 2x4s are easier to fasten to the ceiling, walls, and floor, and you can use butt joints, eliminating fancy saw work, trimming, and fitting.

Skin the framework with ¼-inch plywood, tempered hardboard, or gypsumboard. Doors may be the same material you use for the skin, if the doors are fairly small. For large doors, use prefabricated units or ¾-inch plywood.

Soss hinges or continuous hinges are best for big doors; you can use regular hinges for lighter ones. Use aluminum track for sliding doors. Simply screw it to the framing, and insert the doors into the track. Decorative hardware should match your decorating scheme.

Ceiling treatments: Because of the depth of washer/dryer units, you should consider indirect or overhead spotlighting in any ceiling treatment that you may choose.

The ceiling may be tile, suspended, or gypsumboard. Or you may want to consider a special treatment with structural plastic panels, a skylight, or just open rafters.

In basement or garage laundry centers, the most inexpensive way to finish a ceiling is not to finish it—except for a coat of paint or penetrating sealer/stain.

In a closet, bathroom, master bedroom, or on a landing, you'll probably have to install a ceiling for a finished look. For new construction, if you have the space, a suspended ceiling is the best choice to hide any venting, wiring, and/or piping.

Insulation and sound-deadening board may be used in any ceiling treatment—especially in basement areas where noise and moisture may be a factor. Ceiling installation techniques are explained elsewhere.

Details and appointments: Venting, wiring, and plumbing are top considerations in any laundry room addition. You usually have to have a building permit for the installation of all three. And, if you don't have the know-how, don't attempt to do any wiring or plumbing yourself. It could prove very costly.

Wiring for the washer and dryer (if electric) should be on a separate circuit running directly from the main fuse box or circuit breaker. It also should be grounded. You can buy grounding devices for a single circuit. If the dryer is powered by gas, you will have to have a professional hook it up. *Do not do this yourself.*

Plumbing can be extended from the main water and drainage system for a laundry area. You should have a soaking tub installed with the water/drainage hookup. Do not connect drainage to a floor drain or sump pump well without professional help.

Where to get help: Weight of appliances and built-ins usually isn't a factor in adding a laundry center. Design isn't too critical, either. However, you may want to consult an architect, builder, or remodeler for design help—certainly for any plumbing, wiring, or structural problems. Your building materials retailer also will be able to help you with design through plan books and manufacturers' literature. Take a walk through several model homes, too, for more ideas.

Most materials for a laundry center addition can be obtained through a building supply center. Also, consult local appliance dealers, general merchandise stores, and speciality stores that handle appliances.

Plan your job: For a simple addition, you'll need rough plans as to space. Wiring for an electric dryer probably will be 220-volts; a washer runs on housepower. Minimum space for a laundry center should be 4x8 feet, if possible; 8x10 feet is ideal. The utilities will give you specifications for gas and water supply/drainage lines.

Glossary

Bolster—a short length of horizontal lumber or timber placed on top of a lally or masonry column to support beams, girders.

Center-hung sash—is a sash that is hung on its centers so the window swings in a horizontal axis, usually to the outside.

Combination doors—are doors that have a removable glass and screen sections so the door may be used for summer and winter protection against insects and cold.

Dado—is a rectangular groove in a board or piece of metal. It also is a special wall treatment in interior decoration.

Door jamb—is a surrounding case into which any door opens and closes. The framing has two upright members. These are called jambs. A header connects both jambs at the top.

Gloss enamel—is a type of paint. It is made with varnish and some pigment so the coating forms a hard, opaque surface.

On center—usually is denoted by "oc." It is a measurement of stud, rafter, and joist framing. The measurement extends to the center of one framing member to the center of another framing member.

Plywood laundry hamper (above) has 1-inch holes drilled in all sides of it for ventilation to prevent mildew. The hamper is on casters, so it can be rolled to the washer. Unit was built from ¾-inch plywood, butt-jointed. It is painted.

Ideas at a Glance

You can incorporate most of the innovations on these pages into your laundry room addition plans to make it the smooth-running center it should be to save you time.

Standard base and wall cabinets you can buy at most building material outlets were used for this laundry center. They're hung on wall studs with screws. Countertop height of cabinets matches the height of the washer/dryer, so the cabinets/appliances can be used for folding.

Dolly with roller skate wheels—similar to a skate board—transports this large wicker basket hamper to laundry appliances. For behind-the-door space, shelves were removed from a prefabricated base cabinet in one corner of a kitchen. The laundry is located across the room in another cabinet area, forming a 'galley' type arrangement.

Simple box of 1x12 dimension lumber was used for storage in this laundry center. The 'doors' are window shades. Standard shade brackets are screwed to the top of the cabinet. The cabinet is fastened to the wall with metal angle brackets and toggle bolts. For deep shelves, plywood could be used for this installation.

Don't bypass the possibility of including an ironing and sewing center in your new laundry plans. All are compatible and may save the homemaker countless steps running to different areas for the separate functions.

With today's building materials, you can enclose your laundry area without danger of damage from moisture. Folding or sliding doors can make the center look like a built-in storage area, if the facility will be located in a family room or kitchen.

Closet was renovated to accommodate a washer and dryer combination—and plenty of storage space (right). The shelves are 1x12 dimension lumber screwed and glued together. Spacing of the shelves was determined by measuring typical laundry supplies and accessories. Standard louvered doors, which you can buy at most building supply outlets, are hinged to the framing.

Partition wall was built out six feet from a foundation wall to create this laundry space. Double header supports an aluminum track for a top-hung sliding door. Shelf is a long length of 1x12 supported by metal shelf brackets anchored to the foundation wall. A fluorescent fixture was installed in the recessed or soffit area over the appliances to provide plenty of lighting.

Special wall with room for hampers and laundry accessories was built next to this washer and dryer (below). The ceiling was painted black; the concrete block walls were painted with a moisture- and mildew-resistant paint. Regular window shutters were utilized for the cabinet door, and they are hinged to 1x12 framing. The cabinet is fastened to one wall and the floor for stability.

A ¾-inch-thick plywood box provides storage for this laundry (right); it is hung from the ceiling with 1x6 boards. The closet pole is fastened to the uprights with metal brackets. Raw edges of the plywood are finished with wood putty, and sanded and painted. Screws are used to hold the 1x6 members to the plywood box, which is assembled in butt joints with glue and screws. Although plywood was used here, the back of the cabinet could be ¼-inch-thick tempered hardboard or a bright piece of plastic sheet.

Cabinet front in this laundry storage cabinet was made into a desk top for a planning center. Shelves behind the desk top hold writing supplies —and laundry supplies, too. A length of chain helps support the weight of the desk top, which is covered with ⅛-inch tempered hardboard for a smooth writing surface. Rest of cabinet is simple plywood framing with a folding door.

Boxlike storage holds an ironing board and laundry supplies on shelving. Two sheets of 4x8 exterior-grade plywood with A-A face were used to cover the 1x6-inch frame, simply hinged together. The shelves are supported by screws from the side rails, plus small metal angle brackets. The unit is fastened to a paneled wall and held together with a friction catch.

Porch Conversion

Look to a porch for more living space, if you can't go up to the attic, down to the basement, or out to the garage. Porches offer you plenty of extra space that usually can be screened or walled in to make it more efficient. If the basic structure is already built, you just have to fill in the blanks with more building materials. Here's how to do it.

Winterizing the Porch

A problem with many older homes is the lack of space for family functions and for entertaining guests. The solution may be found on the porch. This is especially so in climates where porches may be used only several weeks during the year. Insects, leaves, and snow occupy the space the rest of the time.

Not only did this homeowner winterize his back porch, he 'ized' it for spring, summer, and fall, too, by enclosing the space and finishing it into a semiformal living room, shown here.

Construction was not complicated: the porch was framed in, sheathed, and sided. Inside, the old siding was removed from the house and a double-opening created into an adjoining dining area. A small bay was formed with five double-hung windows; French-type doors were installed on each side of the bay to match the architecture of the house. To take advantage of those days that may be spent outside, a flagstone patio was built off the porch into the yard.

The bay in this conversion forms a window seat that may be opened for added storage. The built-ins at the sidewall are used for book storage and fine China.

Floor of the porch had to be raised to match the floor level inside. This was done by adding a low foundation around the porch and framing it in with sills, joists, and a plywood subfloor. There is one step down from the French doors to the flagstone patio.

The living room and dining room are carpeted with the same material, so the hookup between the rooms is not noticeable. The same carpeting, along with the big double-doors, also gives both rooms added dimension.

Expanding Living Space

Porches have a wonderful nostalgia about them: a squeaky swing on a summer's night with the fragrance of honeysuckle heavy on the cool night air. Porches also have a problem-insects. You can have the nostalgia and get rid of the insects with a glassed-in porch addition that also offers more efficient living space. This porch is framed with 4x4-inch posts, a roof, and insulated glass panels and sliding glass doors. The doors have sliding screen panels for summer use.

This porch roof does double duty-it protects the living area below and serves as a sun deck above. Access to the deck is through the double doors in a small bedroom addition. A low fence around the deck offers sunbathing privacy and adds architectural interest.

A circular patio was built around the porch; the patio is elevated about 12 inches and finished off with flagstone strips. The block design of the patio is carried into the enclosed porch area. Same lighting was used inside.

Porch into Utility Area

A big family, lots of friends, and a small kitchen were the space problems here. Cabinets were lined up in typical galley style. The adjoining portico was the answer to more space. The sink and dishwasher in the table are reserved for pots and pans, and they use the same plumbing lines. A second dishwasher is used for dinnerware.

Stretching home improvement dollars is easier when you can take advantage of existing construction.

For instance, this cramped kitchen area was opened up by using a seldom-used portico. The footings, roof, foundation, and brick-lined walls give the room a head start. Another plus was the wiring and heat ducts— already in position and ready for a simple hook-up.

What makes this conversion bigger and better are the open plan, wide passageways, white-paneled walls, and light floor and ceiling. Six may sit uncrowded around the table. Nearby is an alcove that cradles a desk, television set, and books.

Like any kitchen space, your conversion should be planned: here, an island countertop area; and walls with plenty of storage space for appliances, dishes, food, and utensils. Valance lighting supplements the table fixture for overall room lighting.

The conversion involved removing a partition wall, which was not load-bearing. Since the sill for the wall is on the same floor level as the original kitchen, vinyl sheet flooring was used to cover the area. Only minor patching in the floor was necessary.

A new outside wall was built with sliding glass doors that lead onto a deck. The same doors and two of the windows were saved from the old wall for the new.

Select the Right Materials

You may want to convert your present porch or portico into enclosed living space. Or you may want to add a porch onto your home. Either way, you'll find the project easy, if you're a skilled handyman, or not too costly, if a professional takes over.

Standard building materials may be used for either project, and there are no secret tips to success. Keep in mind, however, that the porch has to be solid structurally. Don't attempt to convert an existing porch or build anew without the proper foundation and roof support for the add-ons.

Keep plans on a 4-foot module, if you can. Building materials are based on this increment, and, therefore, are easier and less costly for you or a professional to install.

Floor treatments: You're in luck if the existing porch floor is concrete. Chances are it is thick enough and reinforced to handle the additional weight of the sidewalls. If the floor is flagstone, patio block, brick, or a similar block-like material, you'll probably have to remove this material and put down a new floor with footings and proper reinforcing.

You may be able to convert an elevated wooden porch floor into more living space if light screen panels are used for the sidewalls. Regular partition walls may be too heavy for the underpinnings to support the weight. If you want regular walls you'll have to lay a new on-grade floor or build perimeter foundation walls to support the additional weight. If you are in doubt about which way to go, consult an architect or builder. The extra expense of a professional can save you plenty in the long haul through design short cuts.

A new floor—to replace the old one of bricks, blocks, or flagstones—should be of concrete, blocks laid over a sound subfloor, or a plywood subfloor laid over joists supported by a foundation wall.

You must underpin the floor with piers or a foundation wall that goes below frost line —usually 44 inches or so. Since the floor is new and will be covered, you will not have to pitch it for water drainage. However, it must be smooth-finished.

An existing floor may be pitched slightly for water drainage—especially if it is not covered by a roof. If the floor covering will be laid directly over the existing floor, and sidewalls will be installed, you will have to put down a sill to support the framing. And because the floor is pitched, you will have to level the sills. Use cedar shingle shims for this. The sills are fastened to the floor with lag bolts and lead expansion anchors inserted into holes drilled into the floor. If the floor is wooden, you may spike the sills directly to the flooring. Again, you may have to use shingles to shim the sills level. Don't overlook insulation at sill level; a product is made for this.

Existing wooden floors on brick or block piers may have to be reinforced, since the piers tend to crumble from moisture. If this is the problem, use a screw-jack to lift the porch floor so you can repair the supports. Distribute the weight by inserting a 2x6 between the jack and the joist or support member. Don't overturn the jack; just lift the porch enough so the weight is off the support. You can use this same technique if the supports are wooden. However, you should replace wooden supports with concrete or concrete blocks, as wood, in time, will rot away from moisture. Termites can cause problems, too.

A sleeper block subfloor may be used when the present floor has to be elevated to match entry doors in the house. This consists of 2x4s, 2x6s, or 2x8s laid in rows on edge, then covered with a plywood subfloor. The finished flooring goes over the plywood if the porch will be enclosed, to make it weather-tight. (See the Garage Additions section of this book for details on how to install the floor.)

Indoor/outdoor carpeting is the best floor covering when the porch will be subjected to the elements and you want a decorative effect. If the porch will be enclosed, use resilient flooring, hardwood blocks, hardwood strips, linoleum, shag carpeting, or most any type covering you would like to have.

If your plans call for screening the porch in the summer months and switching to glass panels during the winter, stick with hard flooring materials such as concrete, patio blocks, bricks, tile, and cypress and redwood.

Wall treatments: Wooden and metal columns, posts, and ornamental iron are standard materials to hold up a porch roof. All are part of a wall system, since they provide wall support.

To close in a porch, incorporate the columns into the walls if possible. If not, remove the columns by bracing the roof with temporary posts until you erect the sidewalls.

The first step is to remove any trim pieces covering the roof structure at the underside framing. Go right down to the framing. With a double 2x4 or a 4x4 post, brace the roof structure and take out the porch columns —one at a time. Be sure you brace the roof at each bearing point. Nail the columns to the roof framing and to the floor framing. If the floor is concrete, hold the bottom of the column with a metal pin in the center of it. Here you may have to lift the column up off the pin. In some installations you can embed the column in concrete. If you do this, saw the column flush with the concrete.

Frame the new wall with 2x4s on 16-inch centers. Nail the 2x4s to a header and sill plate. Double them at the corners. If the roof span is a long one, you might have to divide it with a double 2x4 or a 4x4 for additional support.

On concrete, fasten down the sill with lag bolts and expansion anchors on 18-inch centers. The anchors fit into holes drilled in the concrete. If you are placing a new concrete floor, set the sill bolts into the fresh concrete after you screed it, but before you finish-trowel. The threads of the bolts should protrude enough to span the thickness of the sill, plus ½ inch or so.

Frame doors and windows into the walls at the same time you build the walls. Double the headers, jambs, and sills.

Enclosed post-and-beam construction generally involves 4x4 posts, a header, and a sill. Space these framing members to accept insulating glass panels and sliding glass doors. Hold the panels in the frames with 1x1 stops, rabbet them into the edge of the framing, and secure them with outside trim pieces.

Removable screen and glass panels may not need the heavy framing support provided by 4x4 posts on 24- or 48-inch centers. You must, however, provide support for the roof at the main bearing points. Fasten the frames for the panels to a header and sill with 2x4s. Or fasten them directly to the concrete with metal pins. Use redwood or cypress or specially treated lumber to deter rot from moisture.

Finishing materials for conventional porch walls may be gypsumboard, plywood paneling, simulated brick or stone, structural plastic panels, hardboard, or canvas panels. Outside, sheath the walls with plywood or insulation board, and cover with siding to match the architecture of your home.

Screen and glass panels fit in wooden or metal (usually aluminum) frames. You can buy the panels prefabricated or fabricate them yourself from parts.

Insulated glass panels, sliding glass doors with screen combinations, and regular doors and windows may be purchased prefabricated and ready to slip into the framing. But before you build the structure get the measurements of the doors and windows so they fit perfectly. Do not try to force large glass panels into framing members. This could cause a torque in the frames, breaking the glass.

Prefabricated porches or rooms may be purchased at many building supply outlets. You can assemble the units over most any type surface for summer use, then disassemble and store them during the winter.

Ceiling treatments: On existing porches, the ceiling may be open with the framing exposed or covered over with a material such as gypsumboard or ceiling tile. Chances are you won't have to change the structure of the ceiling to enclose the porch. You may want to remodel it, however, with sheet plastic, tile, paneling, or any number of materials available for this specific purpose.

To construct a new roof, either support the rafters on joist hangers nailed to the house sheathing or a ledger strip, or rest the rafters on a ledger strip. You must have support.

If you shingle the roof, cover the rafters with sheathing, asphalt building paper, flashing, and then the shingles. If the roof will be built-up, tar-and-gravel construction, you can frame in the structure, but call in a professional to install the finish roofing. Tar-and-gravel roofing takes special equipment that usually can't be rented or is too costly to purchase for a one-time job.

For heavy roofs use standard 2x6 or 2x8 rafters on 16-inch centers. For lightweight roofs, such as structural plastic panels, screening, or tightly spaced purlins, the framing may be lighter (2x4s or 2x6s), spaced on 24- or 48-inch centers. Ask your building material supplier for load table information. The roof, of course, has to be strong enough to support snow loads—even if it is lightweight.

For flat roofs, you'll need a slight pitch for drainage. Or you can build the drainage system into the roof with connecting downspouts. The roof should have an overhang or eave to protect the sidewalls. You can install gutters and downspouts as on a conventional roof.

Details and appointments: Heating and cooling are important if the porch will be enclosed as part of your home. If the heating/cooling plant has enough capacity, extend the ducts from the main house through outside walls. Otherwise you'll have to add a new unit in the room. Power hook-up is no problem.

Wiring and plumbing in a permanent enclosure also may be extended from the existing system. Consult a professional.

Lighting and convenience outlets for a porch that will not be used year-round must be wired according to outdoor specifications: waterproof fixtures and outlets. Wires must be in conduit. This is necessary by code where wiring will be exposed to weather.

Where to get help: Architects, builders, and remodelers can help you with the design and construction of a porch for your home.

In most areas you'll need a building permit to do any construction work, with the exception of a prefabricated porch room or the installation of light glass/screen panels.

You also may obtain design help from magazines and books. Many building supply retailers have plan books and manufacturer's literature that may help you with both design and detailed construction techniques.

Plan your job: If your porch project is an involved one, seek professional design help. But if the project is a simple enclosure or a tack-on structure, rough drawings should suffice. Either way, most cities will ask you for a plan before they will issue you a building permit.

Space allotment for a porch depends on the size of your lot, the architecture of your home, and what the new space will be used for. As a rule of thumb, you should have at least 8x12 feet of space for the project. Also keep in mind any future expansion plans, landscaping of the lot, and your life-style as to entertaining. Don't skimp, if you have space. Additional lengths and pieces of building material are not that expensive; build the room you need at the outset. It is expensive to undertake the remodeling of a remodeling after a few years because of poor initial planning.

Glossary

Bond—is mortar or another mixture that is used to join bricks or concrete blocks. The mixture also can be used for tuckpointing.

Built-up beam—usually a girder that has been fabricated with several heavy pieces of material, usually wood.

Corner boards—butt against the siding at corners, doorways, windows.

Deck paint—is generally used on porch floors and stairsteps since it has a very high resistance to mechanical wear.

Panel—is a large, thin, board or sheet of lumber, plywood, or other material. A thin board with all its edges inserted in a groove of surrounding material. A section of floor, wall, ceiling, or roof—usually prefabricated in a factory or by a lumberyard.

Pitch—refers to the rise of a roof. The rise is in inches or rise per foot of the total run of the roof. It also may be expressed by the ratio of the rise of the roof to the span of it.

Post—is a timber set on end to support a wall or a floor of a structure.

Ideas at a Glance

A special skylight; super plantings; a window wall overlooking a beautiful view; special spot-lighting; an antique. These and countless other 'details' can make your porch remodeling something special. Let the ideas on these pages show you how you can modify, build-in, innovate, and create.

A skylight in a porch enclosure or addition accents natural light, and, best yet, is easy to include structurally (right). This dome-type skylight was used on shed roof. Hanging plantings thrive well from increased outside light. Glass is fixed in mullions of 4x4s and 2x2s dadoed in the 4x4s. Special ceiling treatment may be created with 1x2s nailed to joists ½ inch apart and stained.

This enclosed porch (below) is ideal for plantings because of sunlight and ventilation. Barn-type siding, with batts to cover the joints, was used on this porch; extension of framing members adds another dimension to the space. The fireplace is a prefabricated unit; the hearth is real brick laid-up over a concrete floor. The dropped ceiling hides indirect lighting.

A porch is a porch—whether it's enclosed or not. Below, a deck-type porch was added, taking advantage of the big roof overhang and a sliding glass door into a dining area. The materials are redwood on a 2x10 frame running parallel to the house. Posts and 2x6s support the joists for the 2x4 decking. The low benches also serve as a railing for safety.

This decorative fan right out of the 1930s is more for show than blow. Ceiling of the porch addition was left open; joists and supporting beams are stained a dark color and protrude beyond the facia for added dimension to the porch. Uprights are 4x4 redwood posts spaced on 48-inch centers. The space between could either be screened or glassed in.

Beam effect is achieved here by boxing in space above the windows with regular framing and gypsumboard. The glass was inserted between 4x4 framing members on 48-inch centers. The 3-foot-square columns are not structural; they are fabricated with a framework of 2x4s and covered with gypsumboard, which is finished with a thin coat of sanded plaster.

This porch/deck (below) extends the visual dimensions of this home. The porch almost could be classed as an addition to the house. It is supported over grade with 4x4 posts on 24-inch centers and double 2x10 joists running parrallel to the 2x4 deck boards. Stringers for steps are 2x12s, which are dadoed into the stringers and supported by 1x2-inch strips.

A garage roof overhang could be extended to create a covered patio area like this one. The ceiling is finished off with gypsumboard and painted with sand-textured paint. The facia and overhang are finished with a plywood soffit and a 1x6 piece of redwood. The lights are hooked in a series, while the alcove for the service bar was built from 1x6 t/g pine.

INDEX